Lesbian Crushes

A Diary on Growing Up Gay in the Eighties

by Natasha Holme

Also by Natasha Holme

Lesbian Crushes and Bulimia:
A Diary on How I Acquired my Eating Disorder
(1989-1990)

Lesbian Crushes in France:
A Diary on Screwing Up my Year Abroad
(1990-1991)

Tuesday 20th December 1983, Home

As this book is very personal, anyone intruding had better stop now.

I want to get this off my chest. Here goes:

At the beginning of the summer holidays I wrote, as usual, a list of things to do before going back to school, one of which was 'try a fag.' GOSH GASP.

One day at the ice rink I noticed a cigarette machine. SHOCK HORROR. Next visit to the ice rink I brought with me two fifty pence pieces. I gave Louise (my sister) the slip and bought a packet, then showed her in the cloakroom. She was quite amazed.

When we got home we went into the woods. I had the first puff.

"Can you see anything, Louise?"

"No. Try harder."

I've bought a fag lighter too and lots of things Mum and Dad don't know about, like deodorant, body spray, and a razor. And I drink rum and brandy from the larder. What a bad girl I am. I'm glad I got all that off my chest.

Saturday 14th April 1984, Girl Crusaders Camp, Canal cruise

The canal boat is lovely. Louise and I are sharing a cabin. In the evening we had a Bible class. Our cabin is messy already.

Sunday 15th April 1984, Girl Crusaders Camp, Canal cruise

We started out for church at 10am. It was a two hour walk. The service was totally boring. Even the leaders didn't like it. Then the two mile walk back again.

Eight miles of cruising today and I got to steer. It was wonderful.

Monday 16th April 1984, Girl Crusaders Camp, Canal cruise

Spent most of the afternoon on my bunk bed reading Smash Hits and watching the scenery go by.

Bible study.

Wednesday 18th April 1984, Girl Crusaders Camp, Canal cruise

After dinner Miss Barnett shouted at Louise for doing nothing to help. Well, she had it coming.

We played games of rounders, then evening prayers.

Miss Grant has got very nice clothes and eyes.

Friday 20th April 1984, Girl Crusaders Camp, Canal cruise

I don't want this day to end. I'd be happy if my life was one Crusader Camp after the other.

In the afternoon we all had to clean the boat.

Prayers. Recorded Camp song. Bed.

Saturday 21st April 1984, Girl Crusaders Camp > Home

The last day. I don't want to go. Everyone's swapped addresses with everyone. Miss Barnett woke us all up at 6:40am so that we could have breakfast and then be first through the locks, which open at 8am.

I'm already missing Camp. Well, I did when I stepped off the boat. Boo hoo.

Sunday 29th April 1984, Home

Haven't smoked for ages!

Matthew Lewis—the true story ...

Here goes:

At the school disco, Louise was dancing with this slob. She couldn't get rid of him, so she sent him to dance with me. He kept pestering me for a fag. I only had one. He said he was desperate, so we went outside to find somewhere private (my heart: thump, thump, thump). There wasn't anywhere. He stood looking at me. I turned cold as ice. He put his head on my shoulder. I said, "Come on," and we went back to the disco.

I slow danced with him and he kept asking me out and I *kept* saying NO.

A few months later some of us arranged to meet up with a few of the Boys' School boys for a drink in the Central Café. One of these boys was Matthew Lewis.

Again he kept asking me out and I kept saying NO ... but then I gave in. He walked me to where Dad was going to pick me up in the square. Then we—you know ... kissed. ... He put his whole tongue in my mouth. I said, "You stink of cigarettes." He left just before Dad arrived. Phew.

Someone gave him my number! So, we arranged to meet a couple of times. We went to the school barn dance. Big deal. It was really exciting, I must say.

At the next school disco we did go outside, but then I chucked him and he went off with Sam Rees.

The most boring months of my life. I'm through with slobs.— There you have it.

Saturday 8th September 1984, Home

UPDATE: I feel just awful when I read all those things back there.

I threw my fags away ages ago.

I do not intend to go out with any non-Christian boys, and I do not drink anything but cider and wine occasionally. Phew. THAT'S BETTER.

Three or four weeks ago Louise and I were at the Aberlour Girl Crusaders Camp. It was fantastic. I am writing to Sharon. She is a really good friend of mine. She cried at the station. She's ever so pretty.

Oh, and I won the table tennis competition again. I won a Balmoral biro. Sharon was better than me, but she got all nervous in the final match. I feel terrible, but she was so nice about it.

No.1 is *I Just Called to Say I Love You* by Stevie Wonder.

Sunday 16th September 1984, Home

Boy, do I miss Sharon?

Yes! ...

Wednesday 10th October 1984, Home

I dreamt last night that Sharon was on top of a bunk bed in her pyjamas at Camps' Reunion, throwing pillows. I saw her for the first time in months and she just said, "Hi Natasha." I almost cried.

Today in maths of was thinking of the way you tell how much you care for people—by imagining how you would feel if they died. I thought about Sharon. Then I thought, 'No, God, please,' and started crying. Luckily I pulled myself together before anyone drowned. I thought about it on the way back from my piano lesson, too—and cried again.

Oh, and *I Just Called to Say I Love You* by Stevie Wonder is still no.1.

Thinking I've got a good friend in Sharon helps me get over Jackie.

Wednesday 17th October 1984, Home

I've had another five or six dreams about Sharon. I'll tell you why, shall I? It's because I don't know how she could like a plonker like me. And I'm just terrified that at Camps' Reunion she might come to her senses, OKAY?

Russell Harty on TV about a week ago was talking about how irresponsible parents leave books about the facts of life around so they don't have to tell their children themselves. Who does that remind me of?

No.1 is *Freedom* by Wham.

Friday 19th October 1984, Home

TODAY was different. At the end of assembly Miss Tennyson asked the Lower Fifth Spanish group to stay behind. We had been accused of writing on the Upper Thirds' desks in room 19.

Miss Tennyson said, "I don't expect you to write 'fuck off' on desks, or 'fucking, sodding bitch,' or suggest that any member of staff is sexually … strange."

We couldn't believe it and we were trying not to burst.

She said, "'Fuck' isn't a word you should use for something that is supposed to be a *beautiful experience*." That was lovely. I nearly fainted. I haven't heard anyone speak so plainly. Especially Miss Tennyson.

Then:

"Do you know what the word 'sodding' means? Hands up if it's just a swear word to you?" (Everyone puts their hands up) "Does anyone know what it means?" (No hands) "Then I presume you use it out of ignorance. It is the most *repulsive* word and I cannot believe you'd use it if you did know the meaning. I suggest you look it up in the dictionary."

I did. It took me ages to find out. It was under 'sodomy.' She wasn't joking. It's disgusting.

Mr. McKay was a quarter of an hour late for Spanish, sticking up for us, arguing with Miss Tennyson. He assured us that no-one was going to get detention. According to evidence, it couldn't have been us who had written on the desks. He told us that someone had also written 'Mr. McKay is a *something something*.' He was lovely about it. He didn't even show being upset. But he added, "I'm not." And we all cracked.

6

I had a talk with Mr. McKay after school for ten minutes about Spanish and French. He knew *everything* about me, that I'd got grade 1 in French and German. He said I was obviously a linguist, that he was really pleased when he saw my "well-known name" on the list for Spanish. I owe everything to Miss Williams. I think she's great.

Right, now I've got to tell you some of the comments people made about what Miss Tennyson said:

Lee: "How the hell does *she* know?"

Sara: "What does *she* know about it?"

Didn't see who: "We've had more beautiful experiences than her."

Monday 22nd October 1984, Home

This is the *most* exciting news: We were in room 19 for Latin today. I had a look at the desks Miss Tennyson had been talking about. The words were:

'Mr. McKay is a GAY WALLY.'

I had to fight to contain my laughter. Isn't he sweet? Couldn't find anything else written on the desks though.

Tuesday 23rd October 1984, Home

George in *Brookside* is going to prison. George was innocent, you morons.

Anyway, I asked Mr. McKay if I could be moved down from group 1 to group 2 for French. I must have Miss Williams teaching me or I won't learn a thing—I mean it. Mr. McKay said he'd have a word with her. Ohhhhh ... I wonder what will happen?

Friday 26th October 1984, Home

We have just broken up for half term. Mr. McKay has told Mrs. Duffield that I want to move from her French class down to Miss Williams's. Mrs. Duffield talked to Miss Williams about it, and has now talked to me about it three times. She said Miss Williams said I should definitely be in group 1.

You'd think Miss Williams would tell me about it personally, wouldn't you? Well, that might have something to do with me trying to avoid her all this week (embarrassing situation). To get to the main corridor she always takes the undercover route. So, I've been going across the playground. Once safely across, I keep my eyes peeled, ready to turn round and go the other way.

Mrs. Duffield asked me if I didn't think she was a good teacher. Just my luck. I knew she'd take it personally. But she does take a lot more notice of me now.

Monday 5th November 1984, Home

I wrote to Sharon. I told her that I love her.

But the real news of the day: I was standing in the lunch queue in the corridor. People were everywhere. Everyone was swearing and telling jokes. Along came Miss Williams. She was wearing this really nice red pullover. She was pushing her way through the people, and I was staring at her. Suddenly she looked at me. We were just looking at each other. It seemed like ages.

Every time she looks at me I try to look rejected (which I have been), but sort of a game really. She's so pretty though, don't you think?

I can't help it, but I've got these games with some of the teachers (except they don't know it):

Mrs. White (biology): She keeps telling me off for smiling too much. She thinks I'm up to something. So, whenever I see her, I give her my cheesiest grin.

Mrs. Duffield (French) and Mr. McKay (Spanish): I try to see how many times I can get them to have a chat with me.

The head of English: I always look for her reaction in assembly. She knows I'm a Christian because we had to write an essay about what we believe.

Mrs. Addison (French): I always feel like I have to prove something to her. I have always remembered the time she questioned me about my arriving at school late. She made a reference to me being a *slow* person (the deep root of all my problems). This stirred me. I did not answer her, but stared her straight in the eyes. Boy, it seems ages when you do that. SHE gave way. So there, Mrs. Addison. I do admire her though. She dresses wonderfully.

Thursday 8th November 1984, Home

No.1 is *I Feel For You* by Chaka Khan.

Parents' Evening.

French:

Mum said she'd got the feeling that Mrs. Duffield thought I was BULLYING her and also that Mrs. Duffield thought I didn't

9

think she was a very good teacher. Oh boy, what a mess. I think I'll have to talk to her about this. Mrs. Duffield also said it was hard to get a smile from me.

Biology:

Mrs. White asked, "Does Natasha still hate biology?"

Mum said, "Yes."

Perfect. I rolled around on the sofa, punching the cushion. Big biology test on everything done this term tomorrow. You know, I should have revised.

Latin:

Miss Halsie said I keep switching off.

Art:

Mrs. Harrison said it was hard to get a smile from me. Are you surprised? Double lesson first thing Monday morning with nothing to look forward to but Latin straight after? And Mrs. Gatwick says I'm "OK" at art, but I'll allow that as we haven't had her long.

English:

I am an "interesting person."

So, quite a good evening's development. I'll spend the rest of the night plucking up courage to talk to Mrs. Duffield, and learning this year's biology.

Friday 9th November 1984, Home

Aaaaaarrrrrggggghhhh. I don't know how I get myself into such a mess all the time. Well, at the end of the French lesson I waited outside the classroom to talk to Mrs. Duffield. She seemed to be in there for ages. I kept thinking about jacking in the idea, but I'd only have to go back later because I felt so guilty. I *cannot* understand how I went through with it. God certainly gave me strength. The conversation went like this:

"Errrr ... Mrs. Duffield ..." (me a mixture of stone and jelly)

Next came my planned speech, rattled off, and all the time I was thinking, 'Am I really saying this?' and 'Oh help, what comes next?'

"I didn't realise until last night that you were upset by the things I'd said to you. ..." (near faint) "... My mum said you thought I didn't like you, and I didn't think you were a good teacher."

"We teachers have to have a thick skin." She said she was joking about my not liking her. (I meant to add, "I *do* like you.")

"It's just that I like Miss Williams *so* much, and I never really thought I'd ever have anyone else teaching me French. ..." (I meant to add, "Miss Williams has done a lot for me, and I'm very fond of her.")

"What you'd really like would be for Miss Williams to teach group 1, isn't it?"

"Well ... YES."

"Your last two marks have been very good. Well, let's just forget it for now, shall we?"

Yes, nod, phew. I also meant to say "SORRY." The thing is, Mrs. Duffield, the more time goes on, the more I like you. You have ten out of ten, but Miss Williams has a hundred. I do want to smile at you. I just feel kind of ... embarrassed?

Sunday 11th November 1984, Home

In the morning Louise eventually started her period.

"Mum, will you come up here a minute?"

Mum twigged straight away and got up to go upstairs, but that pathetic father of mine said, "No, no, you stay sitting down. I'll go." He's so stupid. Mum ignored him and went up.

Wednesday 14th November 1984, Home

No.1 is *I Feel For You* by Chaka Khan.

There was the most perfect programme on tonight: Patrick Macnee was the victim of *This Is Your Life*. They showed clips from all the different assistants he had in *The Avengers*. Diana Rigg is BEAUTIFUL (even now).

Still no letter from Sharon.

Friday 16th November 1984, Home

We got our biology tests back. I got 77%! Mrs. White read the mark out as being one of the best in the class. Once I'd found out she knew I hated biology, I decided it was safe to read through the work once. Childish, aren't I? (I think everyone else is plain stupid.)

Mrs. White was on duty at lunchtime. As she strolled past me, she pulled my plaited rat's tail and walked straight on, not turning back. I liked that.

Saturday 17th November 1984, Home

Sara was supposed to be coming over today at 10am. It and It (Mum and Dad) left the phone off the hook (That really gets to me). As soon as I put it back again, the phone rang (about 9:45am). It was

Sara's mum. Sara was in bed with a cold. Phew. I didn't really want her to come. I suppose I'm too shy.

Went into town. Bought *Sex Crime 1984* by The Eurythmics.

Wednesday 28th November 1984, Home

Today was the day I decided on my aim in life: I want to be a French teacher at my school. Brilliant, isn't it? I love French, I love the school, I love the teachers. And you just see. Wait and see. Isn't it exciting, eh? An Aim!

I was too scared to come upstairs on my own tonight. Boring boor (Mum) just came back from her French class and she's yelling the house down again and chucking in her favourite simile, "like a bear garden." She sounds pathetic though, because she only knows a couple of swear words. Ha! (QUAKE).

Who's going to plait my rat's tail in the morning?

No.1 is *Should Have Known Better* by Jim Diamond.

Thursday 29th November 1984, Home

Started wearing my rat's tail down.

Tuesday 4th December 1984, Home

Miss Williams came into our room at lunch. There were only two of us in there, working. She said, "Do you need all these lights on?" I think I murmured, "No." She turned them all off but one and said, "Is that alright?" I croaked, "Fine."

Wednesday 12th December 1984, Home

In our Greek lesson Miss Halsie asked us what we wanted to do as a career. The other two said: "interpreter" and "text translator." I said, "I wouldn't mind being a French teacher."

Friday 14th December 1984, Home

No.1 is *Do They Know It's Christmas?* by Band Aid.

Last day of term. I had already given a Christmas card to Mr. McKay and to Mrs. Duffield, but having carried Miss Williams's round for a few days, I finally plucked up courage to give it to her today. I knew I'd hate myself forevermore if I didn't. Just in time, too—minutes before the final assembly.

I said, "Miss Williams?" and gave her the card.

She said, "Thank you, Natasha," then WINKED at me. In fact—typical Miss Williams. NEED I SAY MORE? She's so nice, eh?

Hey, that was quite a good term.

Saturday 12th January 1985, Home

For Christmas Sharon sent me a box of paper and envelopes. Guess what I put in my letter before Camps' Reunion? "I'm just working my way through the piles of paper I got for Christmas." I mean, what a wally I am. I've been half killing myself ever since.

Camps' Reunion was great. I hugged Sharon when we met and parted. It was really strange. When we were together it didn't seem like we were ever apart. I really love her, you know.

I hate this book. Every sentence makes me cringe in agonising embarrassment. Yuck, I hate it.

Thursday 17th January 1985, Home

No.1 is *I Want to Know What Love Is* by Foreigner.

Everyone in group 2 French were on about their lesson today. Miss Williams has been away for the last two days. I didn't know why. Apparently they were all mucking about the whole lesson. And at the end, Miss Williams said that they were behaving disgustingly, and that they were the worst class she had to teach (I am glad I wasn't there). She said she didn't expect them to act like that when she'd been to a funeral yesterday, and she burst into tears—so everyone said. I do hope it wasn't her mum or dad. I'm very sad.

Friday 8th February 1985, Home

I am so chuffed. No.1 is *I Know Him So Well* by *Elaine Paige* and Barbara Dickson.

I've just remembered, I haven't said. I saw Miss Williams in town on Saturday a couple of weeks ago. It was absolutely incredible. That morning I was thinking I'd never seen her in town before. And I actually thought that if I went, I might see her there. So, I went. And I saw her going up the escalators in John Lewis. I got the shock of my life. I felt ever so weak. Strange, isn't it? She's just the same outside school. I just don't know. I just *don't* know.

It's so terrible when you love someone and you can't tell them. That's what's doing it, you know. I don't really know what to do.

Thursday 14th February 1985, Home

Just to let you know, in the last two or three days, I've been called, by people at school:

- Peculiar
- Polite
- Graceful
- Artistic

No.1 is *I Know Him So Well* by the absolutely beautiful Elaine Paige and the other woman.

Wednesday 6th March 1985, Home

No.1 is *You Spin Me Round* by Dead or Alive.

Would you believe it? I was accused of smoking in the loos by a cross-eyed prefect today. She actually had the cheek to tell me to prove that I hadn't, so I just told her to prove that I HAD. It was quite funny actually. Every person in the year now knows, and Sara keeps mentioning it very loudly when teachers walk past. That girl annoys me.

Miss Williams was away Monday and Tuesday. People are so horrid to her, it makes me cringe. They were saying, "I suppose someone's died?" I just don't understand how anyone could even slightly dislike her. They always say that she annoys them. Oh well, it stops competition.

Sunday 7th April 1985, France, on French exchange

Easter Sunday. Agnès and I went to a Catholic church. It's dead weird. There were four boys standing on the platform behind the vicar bloke. They were wearing great big white cloaks and clunky wooden crosses, with jeans and trainers underneath, and just mooched around looking bored.

We had to sing, most of the time without books. Not hymns—chants, and everyone knew the words except me. There was a woman on the right of the stage leading the singing and waving her arms furiously in the air.

They swung incense round everywhere—just missing two nuns. No, not really. There were a few people coughing, which made the situation even funnier, and I just couldn't help laughing. Later the vicar got a bucket of water and a ladle and started walking down the aisle, soaking everybody. Even Agnès started laughing then.

We had to get up and were given a biscuit thing each—about the size of a ten pence piece. I kept mine in my hand until we got outside, which Agnès thought was funny. I started to nibble it, but Agnès told me to put it on my tongue. Yuck. It tasted like polystyrene.

Thursday 11th July 1985, Home

No.1 is *Frankie* by Sister Sledge.

Miss Williams's form have been collecting KitKat wrappers for their form effort. At lunchtime I was sitting with Louise at the back of the dining hall, opposite the conveyor belt. I had Louise call Miss Williams over and give her my eleven KitKat wrappers. Miss Williams said thank you. Louise said, "They're not mine, they're my sister's." Miss Williams said, "Thank you, Natasha."

Friday 12th July 1985, Home

End of school year.

Saturday 13th July 1985, Home

Got my ears pierced.

Live Aid.

Monday 29th July 1985, Home

Got my ears pierced again.

Thursday 1st August 1985, Home > Girl Crusaders Camp, Pitlochry

I was nervous about seeing Sharon again, but not as nervous as at Camps' Reunion by miles.

Saturday 3rd August 1985, Girl Crusaders Camp, Pitlochry

Played table tennis with Sharon. She won twenty games, I won seventeen.

Sunday 4th August 1985, Girl Crusaders Camp, Pitlochry

Baptist church in the morning—very funny.

Wednesday 7th August 1985, Girl Crusaders Camp, Pitlochry

Sharon was in a real mood. She kept going off on her own, not speaking to me or anyone. I was in tears and the only place I could be alone was the stage in the gym behind the curtains up from the table tennis tables. I must have been up there for an hour or two. It was like we weren't friends anymore. The more I thought about it, the more I cried. No letters, no nothing. I wouldn't be able to live.

Sharon never even asked where I'd been. She was in the same mood in the evening. I was looking for her everywhere. I found her all on her own in the library, reading her Bible.

I asked her, "What's the matter?"

She said, "Nothing."

I sat down in silence. Sharon kept reading her Bible and didn't say anything either. I sat and stared at the wall because I knew she was looking at me. It was horrible. We just sat there. After about TWENTY MINUTES, tears started to run down my face.

She said, "Hey?"

"What?"

"Look at me."

"No."

She came over and sat on the arm of the chair, put her arm round me and said, "I'm sorry."

We were in there for ages. It was awful. I kept thinking it was the end.

Miss Pratt shone a torch under Liz's bed. Sharon and I had left a blanket under there.

Thursday 8th August 1985, Girl Crusaders Camp, Pitlochry

Miss Pratt told us to sleep in our own beds tonight.

Sharon and I slept under Eleanor's bed.

Friday 9th August 1985, Girl Crusaders Camp, Pitlochry

Sharon bought me a pair of silver cross earrings.

I let Sharon beat me at table tennis to put her in the right mental state to beat Miss Jones, so that she would get through to the final with me. She THRASHED Miss Jones. She was SO happy. I said, "I'll have to try and depress you by tomorrow."

I suggested a mock final. The score reached 20:20.

Sharon said, "Let's leave it there."

I agreed.

Saturday 10th August 1985, Girl Crusaders Camp, Pitlochry

For several days I've been suggesting we refuse to play the table tennis final. But Sharon wanted to. I was upset because I knew I was going to win. And I knew equally well how she would react when I did win.

We won one game each. Then I won the third, 21-19. The exact second I won the last point Sharon slammed her bat down and walked off without a word. She doesn't know how much that hurt me.

When no-one was in the dining room I tore the table tennis tournament sheet in half and put both halves on the table. I felt really pleased as I tore it because it was coming between us.

Sharon went into Pitlochry instead of listening to Miss Booth-Clibborn's piano recital. At the end, Miss Booth-Clibborn gave her talk. She said, "Those you love turn against you, but God loves you forever." I couldn't stop crying. I was very angry too. Does she honestly think I would have acted like that if she'd won?

She said "Sorry" to me later, and she said, "I'm never going to play table tennis again."

Sunday 11th August 1985, Girl Crusaders Camp, Pitlochry
The ripped table tennis sheet had gone, and nothing was said.

Sharon and I slept in the middle of the dormitory floor. Miss Jones said nothing. Miss Pratt came in later and told us to get back to bed.

Monday 12th August 1985, Girl Crusaders Camp > Home
On the train journey back to London we played cards. Mum picked Louise and me up. Sharon went home in a taxi. We didn't cry.

Friday 16th August 1985, Home
No.1 is *Get Into The Groove* by Madonna. Madonna married Sean Penn.

Tuesday 20th August 1985, Family Christian holiday, Capernwray

Went to the loo in the middle of the night. When I woke up in the morning, I found myself in bed with Esther.

Friday 30th August 1985, Home

Wore a skirt for a whole day. My my!

Friday 6th September 1985, Amsterdam

Mum was in a right mood because she saw that Dad had written a postcard to Grandma (his mum).

Tuesday 10th September 1985, Home

Back to school: Upper Fifth.

Didn't like school. All plans falling apart. Miss Williams is not teaching French? Miss Peterson is. Help me, someone. I'll kill whoever did this. What's going on? Sometimes I want to die.

Friday 13th September 1985, Home

No.1 is *Dancing In The Streets* by Mick Jagger and David Bowie.

Spoke to Miss Williams today. I nearly fainted. She's so wonderful. I really love her. I'd lost my Spanish vocabulary book, so went to the staff room to find Mr. McKay. One of the teachers was going in there and Miss Williams was walking straight after her. I asked the first teacher if Mr. McKay was in the staff room. It was

Miss Williams, not the other teacher, who came back out. Why??
Miss Williams told me he wasn't in there. She said he would
probably be in the room in which he was last teaching. I said, "OK,
thank you." I was literally shaking. It's so strange, but what do I do?
YES, what DO I do?? * More * Help * Please. *

Another strange thing: I was talking to Kerry Evans at
lunchtime. She went on about how "weird and odd" I am—working
in the lunch hour, never going out at nights, not "socialising." She
said she would have expected me to be "sociable" because I was
"trendy" (!): "trendy shoes with lots of zips and buckles, spiky hair,
and two lots of ear piercings." Wow. And she went on and on about
it. After any comment I made, she said: "Weird. You are soooo
weird." It was really funny.

Friday 20th September 1985, Home

Spoke to Miss Williams again. I was shaking again. I really can't
help it. I was dawdling this morning walking into school so that she
was following me. I opened the door into the main corridor from the
playground for her, and smiled.

She said, "Oh Natasha, do you know who teaches Louise
French now?"

"Um ... Mr. McKay."

She told me that Louise's French exercise book was on her
shelf.

SHE lightens my life. I love her.

Thursday 26th September 1985, Home

I opened the door for Miss Williams. She said, "Thank you, Natasha."

Friday 27th September 1985, Home

Miss Williams asked me, "Was it your book I kept getting, or your sister's?"

"My sister's."

Sometimes I feel like she tries to talk to me, but that's only because that's what I'd like to think.

Saturday 28th September 1985, Home

I've just finished drilling these six holes through this book. Pretty good, huh? Bought padlocks from the market.

Thursday 10th October 1985, Home

Detention for not going to hockey. Do the PE teachers have any idea of how many people also didn't go???

Saturday 12th October 1985, Home

I'll start with last night's dream: I'd heard lots of rumours that Miss Williams was dead. I kept crying, especially when I thought of an eternal life without her. I refused to believe it, and kept looking for her. I was in one classroom and *Miss Peterson* was in another. Miss Peterson called me over and said, "I've noticed that every time I go to the loo, you do too. *I've* got dysentery. That means so have you. So, if you see me in a room, don't come near." I then tried to assure her that I didn't have dysentery. As if to prove that I did, she said, "Lie down with me." I stepped right up close to her and said, "I beg your pardon?" It was really a very good dream. A bit perplexing.

Mum just bluntly refused to let me go caravanning with Sharon. I can't believe it. Why are people treating me like this when I've done nothing wrong? She said there were really strange people on caravan sites, but wouldn't explain any further. What does she mean?—Homosexuals? She said I might get murdered. I assure you, World, I have no intention of dying.

Monday 21st October 1985, Home

Louise's cookery teacher. ... What elegance. What style. What beauty. What next? Or more to the point, who next?

Friday 25th October 1985, Home

Today was a terrible day. I don't know quite how to explain it. The question was, "Do I still love Miss Williams?" The thing is: Miss Peterson. I haven't told you about Miss Peterson, have I?

I heard that Miss Peterson was teaching group 2 because Miss Williams couldn't stand group 2 any longer. I thought, 'Well, whoever Miss Peterson is, I don't like her.' I thought she'd be some old bag. I kept trying to dislike her. I kept staring at her as if judging her. And she kept catching me staring at her. Oh dear. Does she remember? I hate not knowing answers.

Thing is, I never disliked her. It was just the thought that Miss Williams was being hurt. I wondered whether they were making Miss Williams stop teaching certain classes? I wasn't being serious, because I knew it wasn't fair. Gradually I liked her more and more. I was trying to fight it, but I failed. I don't know. I never do. She's straight from teaching college, I expect. How sweet. ... It's so strange, as if I feel like I am her. Like she *is* already what I am aiming everything in my life to be. This is awful because previously I thought of Miss Williams in this place. Miss Peterson is so young, so NICE. I love nice people, I'm afraid.

It's horrid, like she's taking Miss Williams's place. But she never could. I keep crying about this. I keep imagining I don't care for Miss Williams anymore, and every time I think this, the tears come, which means I want to keep on loving her, which means I DO love her, which means everything's OK.

On Monday Louise told me she'd been moved down a group from Mr. McKay's class to MISS PETERSON's class. At first I didn't believe her. I even got her to ring one of her friends so I could ask her. When it was proven beyond doubt, I was delighted, thrilled. ... A connection.

Louise was upset about being moved down a group and got Dad to ring up school. The head of French arranged a meeting with Mum and Dad. Thankfully, she's now permanently moved down. The head of French said that Louise had a sister, didn't she? And that he remembers marking one of my papers once. He said that it was "exceptional."

... Exceptional. That makes me so happy, so happy, so happy. It makes me want to cry. My immediate thought is always Miss

Williams. I'd honestly be in group 4 or 5 if she hadn't cared so much. She really is wonderful, you know.

I've just been in my bedroom, thinking this lot through and crying—which means it really IS important. It needed a lot of thought. I just discovered that yes of course I love her, and always shall. It's just that I have become so despairing. Just today. Everything was fine yesterday. But today I thought I'm fed up of this. Two years—two years—TWO YEARS since Miss Williams has taught me. I never thought it would be this long.

Monday 18th November 1985, Home

English language O Level. Mr. Gilbert was walking up and down the rows, looking to see if we had anything we shouldn't. He picked up my huge polythene bag of wine gums and jelly babies and held it up to show the other teachers. They thought it was pretty funny. Miss Gordon, our Latin and Greek teacher, said I'd have to watch it as Miss Williams was coming to sit next to me and might get hungry.

My heart skipped its usual beat and I looked round. There she was, giving out the papers. She ended up sitting at the front and one of the other teachers sat at the desk by my side. This is probably a good thing as I'd be too nervous and self-conscious.

Miss Williams was wearing grey boots and a light brown cardigan. I was dead glad when she left.

Wednesday 20th November 1985, Home

Miss Peterson was wearing a gorgeous long beige coat. I like her bright blue cardigan and blue and white horizontally striped top. I really like Miss Peterson. It makes me kind of jump when I see her though.

Thursday 28th November 1985, Home

ONE YEAR since I decided on my aim in life. I am determined from now on to celebrate this day with a bottle of wine. Yes, seriously. I only thought of it today or yesterday, so I've had to settle for a can of shandy—in a wine glass, of course.

Today we were on the bus, talking to Caroline Taylor, one of the Upper Thirds. I asked her who her favourite teacher was.

"Am I allowed to have two?"

"Yes."

She said, "Miss Williams and Miss Peterson."

Thrill. I said, "REALLY?—Who most?"

She thought for ages and decided, "... Miss Peterson."

I said, "That's the wrong answer."

Louise asked Caroline, "Do you know what a lezzie is?"

Caroline shyly said, "Yes."

"What is it, then?"

"It's two women who love each other."

We said: "How sweet."

Tuesday 10th December 1985, Home

I got 99% in the French test. I was so happy. I had thought that everyone was going to get about 100% seeing as we only had to learn forty-four irregular verbs. Not many people did very well at all, and Mrs. Duffield was very disappointed and a little angry. She said that

I made her very happy. She reached inside her handbag and brought out some chocolate for me as a reward, and the class said, "Aww."

I felt happy right up till before the last lesson of the day when I smiled at Miss Williams and she didn't smile back. That kills, no joke. I was on the verge of crying in the last lesson. I cried all the way home. When we got home Mum was trying to find out why. I went into my room and locked the door and cried. Will everything work out? I don't know.

Louise came up and told me that Mum had asked her if Miss Williams was leaving school, because that was the only reason she could think of for me crying. I couldn't believe my ears, and came to the conclusion that Louise was lying.

Wrote Christmas cards today. All except one—the musical Christmas card I bought for Miss Williams from Harrods.

Friday 13th December 1985, Home

I don't much enjoy writing in this book. Well ... I did it. I don't know quite how—definitely a little divine intervention. It was nearly 10:20am and I was walking from the maths room to room 8. I had my Christmas card for Miss Williams tucked in a pile of books and I saw her coming from the playground towards the door into the main corridor. She was talking to one of the teachers. I thought, 'Now or never,' and somehow said, "Miss Williams?" as she was walking through the door. She carried on speaking to the other teacher for a second or two, and then turned to me.

I just gave her the card. I noticed she was wearing make-up— mascara particularly. I can't quite understand, or rather decipher, her reaction. It seemed to me that she was more interested in her conversation. She said, "Thank you, Natasha," but I don't think she winked this time.

She was wearing an apricot-coloured top. I was pretty well shaking afterwards.

After school Mum took me to the wine bar. As cool as anything she asked, "Are there any teachers leaving this term?"

I thought that was a strange thing to ask and said, "No," then immediately tensed up as it clicked. I couldn't believe that what Louise had told me was actually true. I had had no idea that Mum even vaguely knew anything of the sort. I think it was mean of her to risk me getting upset by the answer, just to satisfy her curiosity.

Monday 3rd February 1986, Home

I was very worried about my French. It was a hard exam. I tensed up when I saw Mrs. Duffield before the French lesson. She said, "Natasha, can I be the first to congratulate you on an *excellent* mock." I nearly died with relief. I came top with 81% (2% down from last year, boo hoo). Not bad though, I suppose. Oh, I'm soooo happy. I came top. That's all that matters. And just think, if it hadn't been for Miss Williams I'd be in group 4 or so now.

Next Monday MISS PETERSON is coming to teach us for an *entire* lesson. This is wonderful. I so wanted to know how she teaches. I can't wait. How funny. Isn't life good?

Thursday 6th March 1986, Home

On the bus Caroline Taylor told me that she'd asked Miss Williams, "If you're sixteen, which year are you in?" Miss Williams said,

"Upper Fifth." And Caroline then asked her, "Do you know Natasha Holme ... the one with the spiky hair?" (which I think is absolutely brilliant). Miss Williams replied, "Yes." Caroline then asked her, "What year's Natasha Holme in?" And Miss Williams replied, "Upper Fifth." I couldn't get all the facts, like Miss Williams's facial expressions, which make much more sense than words.

Caroline thought my questions were strange. She said, "Why are you so bothered?" Annoyingly, Louise was sitting right behind us and you know what she's like.

I really desperately want to trap Miss Williams somewhere and say "Sorry." Do you know, I think I really shall, if I get the chance. I have this feeling that something's going to happen soon. It's got to. I'm going insane. Help!

Tuesday 25th March 1986, Home

Today was one of the happiest days of my life. Miss Williams spoke to me. She hasn't for three months, one week, and five days.

In assembly Miss Tennyson read out the results of Miss Williams's Upper Third form effort: 'Guess how many chocolate eggs are in the jar.'

My heart was beating really fast. ... First prize ... second prize ... third prize. None of them were me. Then Miss Tennyson said, "And special prize goes to Natasha Holme." I nearly died. Sara, who was sitting beside me, said, "You prat. You didn't go in for that, did you?"

I had guessed every number from sixty to a hundred and sixty eggs. The number was ninety-seven. I was dead worried it would be more than a hundred and sixty. Apparently eight people guessed ninety-seven.

We had to go to Miss Williams's room straight after assembly. I wasn't THAT nervous, more excited, I suppose, like it was a challenge. WORRIED more than nervous.

One of the prize winners was in her room, and all of Miss Williams's Upper Thirds were crowded round, but I didn't go in. I just waited outside.

It's really strange—I can't exactly remember what happened. She just seemed to appear in front of me, really suddenly, and hand me a box of Dairy Box chocolates, and then she put a napkin with three Cream Eggs in it on top, which rolled off onto the floor. Oh dear. Was she slightly nervous?

I can hardly remember what she said. It was maybe, "Thank you very much for supporting us so well." And she was smiling. I was grinning all over my face. I kept thinking about the musical Christmas card the entire time.

I gave Caroline Taylor and her friend a Creme Egg each, but I'm keeping the other one and the box of chocolates FOREVER.

It's really strange, as if it never happened. But I was dead happy all day.

I half smiled at Miss Williams in the corridor at the beginning of break. She smiled at me, and I sort of put my head down and smiled back at the same time.

In the French lesson Philippa called me over to show people the stitches I've sewn in different colours of cotton through the skin on my fingers. She was shivering, as she keeps doing. Philippa said, "Show Mrs. Duffield." I said, "NO," because I really didn't want her to see.

Philippa: "Mrs. Duffield, come and have a look at Natasha's hand."

Mrs. Duffield had the strangest look on her face yet. It was classic. Absolute horror. Everyone cracked up at the look. Mrs. Duffield said she always thought I was a "sensible girl." I'm not quite sure what that's supposed to mean. I suppose it's quite funny.

I had a terrible thought this evening: I don't think I said anything to Miss Williams—which means I can't have said "Thank you." Oh dear.

Last day of term tomorrow. I hope something happens.

Saturday 28th June 1986, Home

Got my left ear pierced three more times.

Bought red, yellow, blue, black, white one litre tins of paint. Started painting my ceiling black.

Friday 4th July 1986, Home

Got far with my bedroom mural.

Saturday 5th July 1986, Home

Martina.

Monday 7th July 1986, Home

Watched tape of Wimbledon.

Tuesday 8th July 1986, Home

Watched tape again.

Monday 14th July 1986, Home

Bought *Teach Yourself German* and *Teach Yourself Italian* books. Bought The Velvet Underground LP and Sex Pistols LP.

Friday 18th July 1986, Home

Finished bedroom mural about 2am.

Sunday 20th July 1986, Home

Mum and Dad and I went to London by car to meet Delphine, my French exchange, at Victoria. We walked Prince Andrew and Fergie's royal wedding route.

Wednesday 23rd July 1986, Home

Watched royal wedding on TV.

Thursday 24th July 1986, Home

Bob Geldof's honorary knighthood.

Saturday 23rd August 1986, Home

Got O Level results today.

Came back from Girl Crusaders Camp yesterday. I am so sad. If I have another Camp, I shall have a nervous breakdown. I love Ruth. She's fantastic. I dreamt about her, so she must be. I'm so sad, but that's OK because I'm only happy when I'm sad.

I spent last night crying because I miss Camp so much. I couldn't stop. It's only through love that I'm so sad. Surely that's wrong?

How did I know that Ruth played the cello? Weird. Because if I love someone, I know their mind.

I don't really know what else to write about Camp. I just want to explain more about Ruth. She is nineteen, a vicar's daughter, and she's lovely. I never really said goodbye to her because I had no idea what she thought about me.

Anyway ... my O Level results. I needn't write them as I shall remember them forever.

Oh, why didn't I just say something to Ruth, tell her that I'd miss her or something? Anything. I totally botched it up. Maybe one day I'll meet her again and everything will be OK.

I won the table tennis ladder. Got a Chocolate Orange. Have saved the last piece and shall eat a crumb a day till Camps' Reunion.

Wednesday 10th September 1986, Home
First day back at school.

Thursday 19th October 1986, Home
One of the teachers said something that might have meant one of the other teachers was gay, so added: "Not in an unpleasant way."

Tuesday 18th November 1986, Home

Miss Williams asked me at lunchtime whether I was queuing for salad or for a hot meal.

Friday 28th November 1986, Home

Two years since I decided on my aim in life.

Tuesday 9th December 1986, Home

Learnt that Miss Williams has two sisters and a brother. I can't believe it. I had assumed it was only her. I shall never get over it— never. It hurt to realise that I really don't know anything about her.

Wednesday 21st January 1987, Home

My life is shattered and my final hopes are dashed. I am Mrs. White's form prefect. This means that I can't be Miss Williams's form prefect.

Tuesday 24th February 1987, Home

Mrs. Rodd, our new French teacher, was on duty in the dining hall. I had poured water down myself. I asked her for a hairdryer. She said to me: "Weirder and weirder," then walked off.

Wednesday 4th March 1987, Home

1. God

2. Miss Williams
3. French
4. Sigue Sigue Sputnik
5. Art

Thursday 5th March 1987, Home

Miss Williams gave me a horrible look in the dining hall. I can't stand it, but who can blame her?

Monday 9th March 1987, Home

Went to Christian Union for the first time, with Kate.

Opened the door for Miss Williams. She said, "Thank you, Natasha."

Monday 16th March 1987, Home

Opened the door for Miss Williams. She said, "Thank you, Natasha."

Thursday 30th April 1987, Home

First Italian evening class.

Friday 1st May 1987, Home

Asked Miss Gordon for Italian exam papers as she is head of exams. I was on duty at break in the main cloakroom. Was sitting there looking at the exam papers when Miss Williams walked past. She must have seen. ...

Monday 11th May 1987, Home

Saw Liz talking to Miss Williams after school. I went up to our form room in a mood. Liz came up. It was just the two of us in there. She asked me what the matter was.

I said, "I can't tell you," implying that it was her fault, but not cruelly.

"Tell me what I've done."

"You'd only feel guilty and it's not your fault."

"I won't, honestly."

"... It's just every time I see you talking to Miss Williams ..."

"You wanted to be her form prefect, didn't you?"

I said, "You're everything—German, French for Business, form prefect. I'm nothing."

I was crying and hugging Liz. I told her the only reason I was learning Italian was to try to get lessons from Miss Williams.

"Why don't you ask her to give you some Italian lessons?"

"I can't."

"Why not?"

"Because she knows that I'm doing it to be in her class."

"No, she doesn't."

"She does. I kept asking to go down to group 2 French. She doesn't like me."

"Miss Williams doesn't dislike anyone."

"Maybe she doesn't dislike me, but she certainly doesn't like me. ... I bet you think I'm really stupid, don't you? ... You don't understand."

"No, I don't suppose I do."

I wish I hadn't said anything.

Thursday 14th May 1987, Home

Second Italian evening class.

Friday 15th May 1987, Home

Miss Tennyson was guarding the conveyor belt at lunchtime. She told me off for leaving food when she had expressly warned us NOT to in assembly.

Tuesday 19th May 1987, Home

On duty at lunchtime, counting people in with Kate. Miss Williams talked to me. ... She asked me to find out if anyone wanted hot meals, and told me to get them in more quickly (ouch). I love her.

Thursday 4th June 1987, Home

Third Italian evening class.

Miss Williams spoke to me THREE times. I was counting people into lunch, opposite the maths room. She told me which years to get in. Then twice, at different times, I opened the door for her and she said, "Thank you, Natasha."

Thursday 11th June 1987, Home

I was counting in the first lot opposite the maths room. Miss Williams spoke to me and she didn't even have to. She was just going into lunch and told me which years to let in.

Joy

Friday 19th June 1987, Home

Italian oral exam.

Monday 22nd June 1987, Home

It struck me at the weekend that the Italian essay titles on the past exam papers were written in the 'past definite' tense, not the 'perfect' tense. ... I didn't know any past definite. I asked Miss Gordon about this. She checked with the syllabus, but it didn't say. She told me to ask Miss Williams. I wailed, "Nooo." She kept persisting and I kept begging her to ask Miss Williams for me. She said she wouldn't. But I caught her after school and she said she had done. I knew she would. Miss Williams didn't know, so had gone home to find out. Spending her evening doing something for me? I like it.

Miss Gordon said that she and one of the other teachers had been having a nice little talk about me. Miss Gordon has been saying things like this to me for ages. I asked her if talking about me was her hobby. She said she had been testing me. Mum had said at Parents' Evening that I was moody and grumpy and Miss Gordon had agreed. She was saying these things to see if I would fly off the handle. I have passed with flying colours. She is going to write something in my file about it. In my file, I am "assertive."

Tuesday 23rd June 1987, Home

Phoned Miss Gordon this evening.

"It's Natasha."

She said, "Oh Hello, Holme," which I thought was funny. She's dead nice.

I asked her if she knew which tense yet. She said Miss Williams was finding out this evening and I was to go to the staff room first thing. Oh yeah!

Wednesday 24th June 1987, Home

At lunchtime I got Michelle to sit with me right down at the other end of the dining hall from where the teachers sit, and round the corner. Slightly obvious I was hiding? ... Half ... way ... through ... my ... roast ... I ... heard, "Oh, it *is* Natasha. I've been looking for you everywhere, pain." ... Miss Williams called me "pain." But in a really friendly way. She's lovely.

She always looks different when I see her close to. She told me she thought I ought to use the perfect tense. She was just discussing it with me. She didn't seem in any hurry to go. She said "Good luck" and she asked me to show her the exam papers afterwards. I love her. I felt so unbelievably happy. Adore adore adore.

Thursday 25th June 1987, Home

Good Italian exam. I gave Miss Williams about three opportunities to stop me and ask how I'd done. But she didn't. I felt really upset. I had *better* make it work tomorrow.

Friday 26th June 1987, Home

At break I was waiting at the staff room—on purpose of course—to ask Mr. McKay something. Miss Williams came up and said to me, "Your tense was alright, wasn't it?" meaning that there was no past definite in the essay title. I replied, "Yes, I know," which was a daft thing to say. Then a girl asked her to see if someone was in the staff room and she disappeared.

Grease play rehearsal 4pm till 6pm in the music school. I am playing Miss Lynch, the headmistress. Finished early, so while I was waiting for Dad to pick me up I went up to the modern languages room and wrote on the blackboard:

Miss Williams

is the

GREATEST

What a crease-up.

Started teaching myself German.

Monday 29th June 1987, Home

Went into the French room last period. Wrote "Miss Williams rules OK" on the blackboard.

Thursday 2nd July 1987, Home

The languages tape-work room was locked. I went to the staff room and asked a lady from the office if the head of French was there. I was talking to Karen. She knew I wanted the key, so she added, "Or anyone in the modern language department?" The lady said, "Miss Williams is in there" and went back in.

 Miss Williams came out, saw me, and looked worried and confused. For some reason Miss Gordon was standing with Miss Williams. ... and Miss Gordon WINKED at me. ... I think Miss Gordon knows just about everything. And she knows I know she knows. It's ever so amusing.

Saturday 4th July 1987, Camping with Girl Crusaders

MARTINA beat Steffi Graff.

Thursday 9th July 1987, Home

Grease DRESS rehearsal. I was walking from the quad loos and Miss Williams appeared from round the corner. I was in a frumpy blue dress, hefty black shoes, and thick make-up. I realised what I must look like and grinned at her. She smiled back lots.

 At rehearsal Sonia said I looked "fucking gorgeous" with make-up on and that I was pretty anyway.

Friday 10th July 1987, Home

Last day of term. First A Level year over.

Saturday 11th July 1987, Home

Teaching myself German.

Monday 13th July 1987, Home

Teaching myself German.

Tuesday 14th July 1987, Home

More German.

Wednesday 15th July 1987, Home

Telephoned one of Miss Williams's A Level German pupils. Asked her for the titles of the German literature books. Also got her to dictate me a prose to work on. She said I'd never be able to catch up one year into the A Level course.

Thursday 16th July 1987, Home

Finished my *Teach Yourself German* book at last. It took three weeks.

Sunday 19th July 1987, Home

Gave Dad a list of German books to get for me. He just commented that they were German, but said nothing else.

Monday 20th July 1987, Home

Started A Level revision: Spanish grammar.

Thursday 23rd July 1987, Home

Event at the showground. Fantastic. Louise and I spent the majority of the time at the local radio stand. Got on Lunchbox Quiz with Erica Haines. Wow, I love her. Got home and started drawing her a picture.

Friday 24th July 1987, Home

Finished drawing the picture for Erica Haines, and wrote her a letter. She's gorgeous. Love love love.

Saturday 25th July 1987, Home

The lady who owns the furnishings shop is beautiful. Love her. She looks like Miss Williams.

Posted letter to Erica Haines.

Monday 27th July 1987, Home

Phoned Erica Haines to get on Lunchbox Quiz. Spoke to her, but didn't get on. I reckon the answer is a fork. I'll *have* to get on tomorrow … so I hope she doesn't get my letter till after. …

Tuesday 28th July 1987, Home

Phoned Erica Haines again. Spoke to her, but didn't get on. It was a teaspoon. Wrote to her again—a hundred and one suggestions for Lunchbox Quiz.

Wednesday 29th July 1987, Home

PIN number came today. WEIRD: I was going to change whatever number it was to 5829—the first four digits of Miss Williams's phone number. Good idea, huh? And would you believe it? The PIN number was exactly that, backwards: 9285. AMAZING.

Thursday 30th July 1987, Home

Mum was in a right mood because the airing cupboard had broken. She rang Dad to come home. So I fled. Sat in the alleyway and revised Spanish.

Friday 31st July 1987, Home

Erica Haines read out on the radio a list of people who had sent in ideas for the Lunchbox Quiz. She said, "Natasha." Great, eh?

Saturday 1st August 1987, Home > Girl Crusaders Camp, Tirabad

Went straight for the table tennis.

Sunday 2nd August 1987, Girl Crusaders Camp, Tirabad

Church. Long walk. Bible class. Missionary slides.

Tuesday 4th August 1987, Girl Crusaders Camp, Tirabad

Bought at the bookstall: *The Fool* and *The Bible, True or False?* And a bookmark.

Wednesday 5th August 1987, Girl Crusaders Camp, Tirabad

Miss Cooke led the Bible study. Very interesting. About sex and gays.

In the afternoon we went on a car ride.

This evening I asked Miss Cooke if I could talk to her about the Bible study. She said tomorrow!

Thursday 6th August 1987, Girl Crusaders Camp, Tirabad

Had talk with Miss Cooke!! We went to a little town, sat in a café and had a drink. I told her. Honestly! And I cried. She said it used to be called "Pash," meaning "Grand Passion." Sweet, huh? She is now praying for Miss Williams.

Sunday 9th August 1987, Home

Worked on Miss Williams's picture, but got a bit carried away, so I'll have to do another for my French department set.

Decided to start reading the book of Joshua.

Monday 10th August 1987, Home

More German revision.

Erica Haines said on the radio that there's an interview with her in the local paper. I asked Dad to get one for me. He got one. And it did have a photo of Erica. Ooh, she's gorgeous. Love her.

Tuesday 11th August 1987, Home

Finished off *Teach Yourself German* for the second time, but still making loads of mistakes. Help. Now properly starting *Mastering German*.

Played tennis against the wall in the back garden. Broke a couple of flowers. Hope Mum doesn't notice. She'll kill me.

Wednesday 12th August 1987, Home

Lots of German. Played tennis in the back garden. Broke lots more flowers. Played tennis in the road outside.

Thursday 13th August 1987, Home

Finished *Mastering German*. Absolute rubbish. No future conditional or subjunctive.

Monday 17th August 1987, Home

More German. I hope this pays off.

Tuesday 18th August 1987, Home

Renewed German library books. Read a chunk of one of the German literature books. Started working on the A Level German prose.

Wednesday 19th August 1987, Home

Packed for holiday. Finished German prose. Very nervous about tomorrow. Louise doesn't seem to be at all.

Thursday 20th August 1987, Home > France

V. v. v. nervous. I got my Italian O Level result envelope and haven't opened it yet. Louise got five O Levels (grade A for cookery). She's pleased. So are Mum and Dad.

Boat to France.

Friday 21st August 1987, France

We drove two hundred miles. Mum was in a right mood when we arrived. She didn't like it. Haven't opened my result envelope.

Saturday 22nd August 1987, France

Three hundred mile journey. Read German literature books. Got to our hotel. Mum in a mood about the traffic and losing our way earlier.

Sunday 23rd August 1987, France

How am I going to tell Miss Williams that I'm planning on joining her German A Level class when I've missed the first year's work?

Tuesday 25th August 1987, France

Mum was in a real mood this morning about Louise wanting to leave home and me not opening my result envelope. Dad said I had to give it to them. I made them promise not to show me. I was really angry. BLACKMAIL.

Friday 28th August 1987, France

Magic dream about Miss Williams. Went to her house. Weird. Really nice.

Tuesday 1st September 1987, France

Beach. Went to buy some chewing gum. On the way back a strange man tried to get me to go off somewhere in his car.

Saturday 5th September 1987, France

Waitress at dinner looks just like Miss Williams. I love her very much. She's gorgeous.

Monday 7th September 1987, France > Home

At the Little Chef I bought a magazine with Raquel Welch in. She looks like Miss Williams. Back home at last. Started getting stuff ready for school.

Tuesday 8th September 1987, Home

Can't wait till tomorrow.

Wednesday 9th September 1987, Home

Wow. I had been so worried about how I was going to break the news to Miss Williams. Followed her back from assembly, and waited whenever she stopped to talk to someone, so it was pretty obvious that I was waiting for her.

As we were both walking through the same set of doors I said, "Miss Williams?"

She turned round.

"Can I do German A Level, please?"

She looked at me speechless, in total amazement.

I told her that I'd taught myself out of a book.

She said to talk to Mrs. Clifton—the head of German. And she went up to her form room.

Later I saw Miss Williams coming through the alleyway. I said, "Miss Williams, could you look at this German prose I've done, please?"

She put down her handbag, took it, and read it. "Have you done the subjunctive?"

I said I had.

She was slightly impressed, I think.

"Is it *too* bad?"

She screwed up her face and said, "Mmm. ... Not *too* bad."

Strange thing: Miss Williams and I seemed to be talking so normally (It wasn't mystical at all) that I was worried that I was falling out of love with her. But I don't really suppose that will ever happen.

Thursday 10th September 1987, Home

Spoke with Mrs. Clifton. She tried to persuade me not to take A Level German, said I should just do the O Level. I asked her if that would be in a class or would I have to do it on my own? She said that two girls wanted to re-take German, so there would be a class.

But who will be teaching it???

She told me to look in the university prospectus to see if there was anywhere you could study German where you didn't need the A Level.

Wednesday 16th September 1987, Home

Today I had my first lesson for over THREE years with Miss Williams ... and I didn't really enjoy it! ... Argh. I felt like a fly on the wall. I felt really guilty—like I'd conned and wheedled my way into her lesson. ... BUT I did get her to teach me again, if only once. So, at least I won.

Sunday 20th September 1987, Home

We went to visit Grandma (Dad's mum) and our cousins because Mum was in France and wouldn't find out.

Wednesday 23rd September 1987, Home

Put the picture I'd designed for Mrs. Duffield on her shelf, face down on top of a pile of books. I was holding my breath in the main cloakroom, standing on the shoe racks, looking through the window. Pretty funny. She took the pile of books out from under it and just left it, as if it wasn't there.

Thursday 24th September 1987, Home

Same again today. Kept putting the picture I'd designed for Mrs. Duffield on her shelf. And she kept ignoring it.

Friday 25th September 1987, Home

This time Mrs. Duffield came out of the staff room about lesson five or six. She picked up the picture, but just looked puzzled, put it back, and walked off. This happened two or three times. So, I wrote on a scrap of paper, 'Please take me,' and left it with the picture. She came out of the staff room again several times to fetch books from, or put books on, her shelf. She still didn't take my picture though.

Wednesday 18th November 1987, Home

Went up in assembly and shook hands with Miss Byron. Won five pounds for my Christmas card design. I had to squeeze past the piano and everybody laughed.

Thursday 19th November 1987, Home

Went to my old infant and junior school's Christmas Fair this evening. Absolutely wonderful—but small. Saw Mrs. Robinson who taught me in my first year of school when I was five. She's beautiful. She has inspiring mannerisms and an amazingly gorgeous voice. She said she remembered my face, but not my name. She asked me how I was getting on.

Monday 14th December 1987, Home

At the end of the French lesson I gave Mrs. Addison the Christmas card I designed for her. She left the room ... then came back in, having opened it. I wasn't expecting that. She said it was beautiful, and she showed the whole class. *What* a lovely smile she has (Oh shut up, Natasha).

As I gave Mrs. Rodd her Christmas card, Mrs. Addison walked past.

Tuesday 15th December 1987, Home

I loved Miss Williams very, very much today. It was cold and her little nose was red.

Wednesday 16th December 1987, Home

After lunch I went to the staff room with the Christmas card I designed for Mrs. Duffield. Discovered she'd gone home and wasn't coming in again this term.

Thursday 17th December 1987, Home

Asked Mrs. Addison if she would be seeing Mrs. Duffield in the holidays. She asked if I wanted a card delivered. She asked to see it. She thought it was lovely. Mr. McKay came over, and they both looked at it.

>Mrs. Addison: "It's bigger than ours."

>Mr. McKay: "That's just what I was thinking."

Tuesday 19th January 1988, Home, Home

O Level German result came today. At the beginning of break, in the corridor, Mrs. Clifton said, "Congratulations." It was only then that I knew the results were out. I twigged and yelled, "Don't tell me, please don't tell me what I got."

She said, "Alright, but you passed anyway."

Mrs. Addison walked past Mrs. Clifton in my direction and asked me, "What do you think?"

I begged her not to tell me.

She was grinning all over her face. "You want to know really, don't you? I'll go into the staff room and come back out again in three minutes, and if you're still here, I'll tell you."

I left hurriedly and went, trembling, for a walk round school. I arrived back at the staff room area, forgetting what she'd said. Miss

Williams was there, about three metres away. Mrs. Addison kept threatening to tell me, so I put my fingers in my ears. "Oh please don't tell me. You won't tell me, will you? Promise you won't?" I took my fingers out of my ears.

Mrs. Addison was grinning from ear to ear: "Natasha, you got an A."

I was in shock, just sort of bouncing up and down with my mouth open.

"You're not joking, are you?"

"I wouldn't joke about something like that."

She said she hadn't actually seen the sheet, but Miss Williams had—so why didn't I ask her?

We walked over to Miss Williams and waited till she'd finished talking to some girl. Mrs. Addison said, "Natasha did get an A, didn't she?"

Miss Williams replied to me, "Yes, Natasha, you did get an A" in a sort of strange, indifferent, couldn't-care-less tone—which upset me. But I was still absolutely over the moon.

In the afternoon, as I was off to my French listening comprehension exam, Mrs. Duffield and Mrs. Addison were approaching. Mrs. Duffield stopped and said "Thank you very much for the card. It was a work of art." Mrs. Addison laughed under her breath and walked off.

Saturday 30th January 1988, Home

At last went to visit the town where Miss Williams lives. Went with Kate. We saw hundreds of white, red, and blue chequered bags. We asked someone where she got hers from—the 50p shop. So we bought one. And I bought forty-eight packets of crisps for £3.

Sunday 31st January 1988, Home
I visited Louise at her boyfriend Nigel's place for the first time. She cooked us a roast.

Tuesday 2nd February 1988, Home
On duty in the main cloakroom at break. Five minutes after break ended I was standing on the bench, looking out of the window at the teachers' shelves. Miss Williams came out of the staff room and went to her shelf. On her way back she saw me standing there, went up to the window and gave me a puzzled look. I got down and met her at the cloakroom door. She said, "Natasha, what are you doing up there?"

"I'm on duty."

She looked at her watch. "Break finished five minutes ago."

I love her.

Wednesday 3rd February 1988, Home
Open Day at Miss Williams's old university.

We went by coach to visit all the halls of residence. Students showed us round. Then back to the university.

Mr. Wolfe, one of the French professors, spoke to us. A German and an Italian professor spoke a bit too.

We were shown round the library, bookshop, language lab.

I told Mr. Wolfe my German O Level result as he had asked me to let him know. We talked about the course and what results I would need. He told me that Miss Byron had written in glowing terms of my linguistic achievements. He was impressed by my different languages and said it was an honour to have met me.

I asked him if he remembered Miss Williams.

"Why? Is she your mother?"

He remembered her name. He would look her up in his files. He asked some of the other professors. The head of modern languages said he did remember her and that she wrote to him a couple of months ago. He asked me to send her his regards. Mr. Wolfe asked me to send her the French department's regards.

Thursday 4th February 1988, Home

Wanted to give Miss Williams the university French department's regards, so tried to find her at lunchtime. I saw her, but was too nervous, so went to talk to someone on duty instead. Later walked slowly in the direction of the modern languages room. I stood around outside—VERY nervous. ... Miss Williams was talking to two girls in her room, so I didn't knock. Phew.

Monday 8th February 1988, Home

Miss Williams looked so pretty today. I'm going to explode with love for her. She's the most beautiful woman in the world.

Monday 15th February 1988, Home

Sat next to Miss Williams in assembly. She asked to share my hymn book. My hand was nearly shaking. She held my hymn book with her left hand. I held it with both hands. She sings beautifully. She was wearing her olive corduroy skirt, white blouse, grey boots. She is so amazingly pretty.

Thursday 25th February 1988, Home

I have decided that from today onwards, in theory, I no longer love Miss Williams. It hurts too much. I'm not going to stare at her at all or be moody or jealous.

Friday 26th February 1988, Home

I really love Mrs. Duffield. It gets stronger every day. She's sooo lovely ... and beautiful.

Bought *Crash* by The Primitives. I love that song to death.

Monday 29th February 1988, Home

Miss Williams was wearing her olive corduroy skirt outfit, which made Thursday's decision v. v. v. hard.

Tuesday 1st March 1988, Home

Got Green Shields stamp catalogue.

Wednesday 2nd March 1988, Home

Thought I would just go straight into the dining hall with the picture I had designed for Mrs. Duffield tucked inside my pad. I stood around the dining hall talking to Kate, then I went up to her, and said, "Mrs. Duffield can I give you a picture, please?"

She said "Is this one of your masterpieces?"

She was wearing her black cardigan, white blouse, black and white skirt. She asked me if I was going to do anything with art for a career. She said she'd get it framed and hang it in their bedroom. It will match as the bedroom is pink and green.

On the bus home I sat next to Caroline Taylor. I was telling her that she should have asked Miss Williams if she could move to her German class instead of being in Mrs. Clifton's, and that her favourite teacher should be Miss Williams.

Caroline Taylor said to me: "You're in love with Miss Williams."

Thursday 3rd March 1988, Home

I walked very casually to the modern languages room. I usually get there as quickly as possible in order to sit and look at Miss Williams before she leaves. So, today I only saw Miss Williams briefly on the stairs on her way down instead. And I even left the dining hall while she was still on duty!

Monday 7th March 1988, Home

I've made up my mind. I'm going to Miss Williams's university and I'm going to study the same course she did. I'm so happy.

Thursday 10th March 1988, Home

Left for the modern languages room even later today. Saw Miss Williams coming through the door to the playground as I casually ambled along. Left the dining hall even earlier while she was on duty.

Friday 25th March 1988, Home

After final assembly I sat on the window sill in the sixth form block, from where I can see both entrances to the staff room. Waited for Miss Williams to come out of the staff room for sherry with Miss Byron. I took two photos of her back through the glass in the door. She was wearing her black skirt and orange top.

Monday 28th March 1988, France

Crying about leaving school. My life is changing and I can't stand it.

Friday 1st April 1988, France

Dreamt a lot about Mrs. Duffield. Dreamt that next year (boo hoo) I went to the school fair and saw the back of her, and went up behind her and gave her a really big hug around the shoulders. I really love Mrs. Duffield. I miss my O Level French days like anything.

We drove to Mme Plouffe's parents' house in the country. Mme Plouffe's grandmother is there as well. She's eighty-eight and all wrinkled. It's really sweet.

Sunday 3rd April 1988, France

In the night I needed the loo. It's downstairs, so I weed in my soap
box. It went all over the floor. I threw what I did manage to catch
out of the window. Thought there was grass outside. There wasn't.
There's now a stain the size of a manhole on the concrete directly
below my window. I was really frightened. Began to pray earnestly
for rain. Prayed on Jesus's name for a miracle.

Three hours later, after I'd been asleep, I heard a curious
scrubbing sound—my band of angels dancing on the spot with
sandpaper shoes, I thought. The scrubbing sound went on a long
time directly outside my window. I was too tired to get up and look,
but eventually I did. The stain had gone. You cannot imagine my joy.

And in the morning I found out that it had rained during the
night. Wow. ... I felt an incredible sense of nearly believing in
Christianity. Discovered also that this was at the back of the house,
where they never go. Jesus even turned the house round for me.

Tuesday 5th April 1988, France

Bought three packs of chocolate cigarettes. Tried throwing them up
in the air and catching them in my mouth—like Sid Snot. Can do it a
bit. Good fun.

Monday 11th April 1988, France > Home

At passport control I was in the queue behind the weirdest-looking
woman I have ever seen. I'm sure that was a man. Very tall and
masculine, though very thin. Bit of a turn-on, really. I think I'll
marry a transvestite.

Friday 15th April 1988, Home

Haven't seen Louise for nineteen days. ...

Sunday 17th April 1988, Home

Went to Louise's 2:45pm. She let me go on her sunbed for half an hour. Didn't get very brown. Nigel was playing snooker and Louise was in a mood about it. She rang up her friend from college to arrange to go out later. Nigel came back 7:30pm and was very angry that Louise was going out. They had a big argument. He said she was going to chat up other boys and that she wasn't to bother coming back tonight.

Tuesday 19th April 1988, Home

Posted my UCCA form, confirming Miss William's university definitely.

First day of term. Read in the school calendar that the German group isn't coming back from Germany till Thursday afternoon. How on earth am I going to manage till then? It's bad enough being at home, but being at school without her ... There doesn't seem any point in going.

Wednesday 20th April 1988, Home

It's too bad without Miss Williams, so I went to the dining hall straightaway at break with the intention of having a conversation with Mrs. Duffield. She seemed unapproachable, so I left. But Mrs.

Duffield came out after me. "How's the revision going, Natasha?" I was really happy. She came out after me. I love her.

Thursday 21st April 1988, Home
Spent today counting the hours till tomorrow.

Friday 22nd April 1988, Home
That's better. She's back. That was the hardest three days I've ever spent. Now I understand how people who hate coming to school feel. It's getting worse. I can't stand her not being near.

Saturday 23rd April 1988, Home
Went down to the Centre. Bought *Sex Talk* by T'pau. Some people from the New Harvest Church were speaking and giving out leaflets. Sat and watched. Cried. A woman called Yvonne came and talked to me. I said I'd come to church on Sunday.

Sunday 24th April 1988, Home
Visited Louise. We went to see Nigel play snooker.

Dad drove me to church 6:30pm. Bit strange (very strange). Songs, plays, preaching. Rather nice.

Yvonne phoned me.

Tuesday 26th April 1988, Home

Got in a real jealous state today at school (where else?). Miss Williams talks to the head of art, Mrs. Gatwick, more than normal.

Wednesday 27th April 1988, Home

Miss Williams sat down at lunch next to Mrs. Gatwick.

Thursday 28th April 1988, Home

In assembly today I sat and looked at Miss Williams the entire time. It was bliss. She was wearing her navy dress. I can't believe how beautiful her eyes are.

Sunday 1st May 1988, Home

Went to Louise's. She wanted Nigel to help us paint their wall red. He wanted to go and play snooker. They had a massive argument. He went and Louise cried a lot.

Dad drove me to church for 6:30pm.

Wednesday 4th May 1988, Home

Last French conversation lesson ever.

Thursday 5th May 1988, Home

Love Thursdays. She never seems flattered or happy or any reaction except slight annoyance when she sees me looking at her. I can't help it. She's so strange—not like anyone else.

Local elections today. Sheet of ten candidates. Had to put four crosses by the ones you want. I put Green, Conservative, Labour, and Social and Liberal Democrats. Mum wasn't pleased. She said I had an irresponsible attitude.

Sunday 8th May 1988, Home

Didn't go to Louise's or get dressed. Stayed in bed and drew pictures for the teachers. Didn't feel like going to church, so didn't.

Mrs. G. next door eventually came round 8:45pm to ask if I wanted to practise French conversation with her as she'd promised. Thanks a lot, I don't think. She told Dad that my French oral exam is tomorrow. Dad came up and said, "Why didn't you tell us? You just make us look stupid."

Monday 9th May 1988, Home

Wasn't too nervous. The examiner asked me what I'd like to do next year. I said I wanted to stay at school. He told Mr. McKay that someone had said that. Mr. McKay asked me if it was me.

Wow. Do you know, Miss Williams never looked so beautiful as today. She looked perfect. Pink skirt and open-necked white blouse and white cardigan.

Phoned Michelle to make sure she was revising for tomorrow.

Tuesday 10th May 1988, Home

Michelle's and Liz's French for Business oral with Miss Williams in the German room. Practised with Michelle all morning. She's rubbish.

Asked Mandy if I could have her photo of Miss Williams from the German trip. She said she had to take them to a German photo evening, but then I could have it. So happy.

Wednesday 11th May 1988, Home

Yesterday Michelle said she couldn't stand Liz because she was Miss Williams's favourite. And she said that Miss Williams hated her. I told Liz this because I'm a stirrer.

Thursday 12th May 1988, Home

Michelle and Liz said Miss Williams has got a Peugeot 405 because she mentioned it in their French oral exam.

Why doesn't Miss Williams ever smile at me? She always glares, as if she's thinking, "Oh God, not her again." She wouldn't care if I died.

Friday 13th May 1988, Home

Got the sheet of questions for the yearbook.

Monday 16th May 1988, Home

Mandy gave me her photo of Miss Williams from their holiday in Germany. I'm very happy. It's lovely.

Wrote Miss Williams a letter (unsent!). I've been wanting to do that for years.

Tuesday 17th May 1988, Home

Kate, Claire, etc. told me what to write on the yearbook form for 'What will your friends remember you for?':

- having conversations with Mr. McKay
- sewing my fingers up
- inch-long finger nails
- eating forty-eight packets of crisps
- not knowing how to buy a train ticket
- doing millions of languages
- my rat's tail
- loving school
- working too hard

They wanted to read the rest of my form. I wouldn't let them.

People were saying today that Michelle is gay. That rumour had been started ages ago, but I'd forgotten.

In *Prisoner Cell Block H* Doreen got into Lynn's bed. That's lovely.

Thursday 19th May 1988, Home

Opened the door for Mrs. Duffield this morning. She muttered "Thank you" without looking at me. As I was following her, I was thinking, "Why doesn't she ask me about my oral?" As she was going into the staff room, she stopped and asked an Upper Fifth how her oral went. When I was back in the sixth form block, I cried.

Went to the Wimpy with Mum. I asked her who her favourite teacher was at school. She said she had a different one every year. I said, "How fickle of you, Mother." She jumped in like I knew she would, saying, "Your favourite teacher's still Miss Williams, is it?" I reckon she knows more than I've let her know.

In *Prisoner Cell Block H* Doreen got into Lynn's bed and they hugged all night.

Friday 20th May 1988, Home

Gave in my form for the yearbook. Liz saw it. She didn't say anything, but she didn't look happy.

Mum and I were talking about diaries. She said she couldn't believe that I kept one, that she was fascinated.

Monday 23rd May 1988, Home

Miss Gordon wasn't there for Latin today. There was a knock at the classics room door. Who came in?—Miss Williams.

I kept staring at her in disbelief. A dream. She was wearing her navy and yellow dress and yellow cardigan. She asked us if she could borrow a chair. No-one answered her. I wanted to, but I couldn't.

Someone moved an empty chair forward. Miss Williams took it. I didn't watch her carry it. I put my head down and worked.

I was so, so happy. I felt as light as a bird. I am so in love with her. Seeing her so unexpectedly made me delirious all day.

1:50pm I went up to our form room, hoping to catch Michelle alone. I did. Wow. I asked her if she had French next and, "Will you do me a favour?—Do you promise you'll do it?"

She replied, "If it's not *too* ridiculous. ... What? ... Take a photo of Miss Williams? ..."

"How did you know?"

"It doesn't take much guessing."

That's funny.

She said she would. I didn't expect it to be that easy.

End of eighth period Michelle came back and shouted, "There you are, Natasha, I've taken one," giving me back my camera. Everyone in the form room then wanted to know what she was talking about, so she said she'd taken a photo of Miss Williams for me. I was too busy cringing to hear all the comments, but someone said, "Do you want to curl up in bed and kiss it?"

I managed not to go red.

I wonder what Liz thought? ...

Today has been one of the happiest days of my life.

Tuesday 24th May 1988, Home

At lunch with Kate and Claire, Miss Williams walked passed our table. Claire asked me why I'd put Miss Williams as 'What or who will you miss most?' in the yearbook.

"I like her."

"What does Miss Williams teach you for?"

"Nothing."

"Why will you miss her then?"

"She taught me French, German, and she was my form teacher. What's the twenty questions for anyway?"

"Seeing her then triggered off my memory and I just wondered."

After lunch went with Michelle to the careers room, so this was my first opportunity to ask her about the photo.

"What did Miss Williams say when you asked her if you could take her photo?"

"Not much."

I persisted.

Michelle told me that she had asked who the photo was for, and that Michelle had told her.

"I told you not to tell her it was for me."

"Well, she asked."

I found that hard to believe, because you wouldn't guess it was for someone else, would you?

"What did she say?"

"She laughed."

I couldn't believe that either. Then, according to Michelle, she said, "How sweet."

This is really worrying me as it seems so unlikely, and Michelle is such a liar. I kept asking her the same questions and she got really annoyed and walked off.

Back in our form room I told Kate and Claire that Michelle was in a mood with me. Michelle replied *not* moodily, "Well, you should stop asking silly questions about Miss Williams."

Louise was at home because Charlie, her budgie, had died.

Wednesday 25th May 1988, Home

Asked Michelle if she told Miss Williams that the photo was for me before or after she took it. She said she took the photo before. Michelle was really annoyed with me.

Thursday 26th May 1988, Home

Miss Williams was not in the modern languages room. She wasn't on duty in the dining room either. It makes me feel really sad. It's 2:44pm and I haven't seen her yet today. I haven't seen her eyes.

And Claire told me there was no assembly today. Assembly is only on Mondays and Thursdays.

Since Monday I had been deliriously happy. But with all this, my heart is heavy again. I look forward to Thursdays so much.

Liz and I were alone in the form room. I quizzed her about Monday. She said that Michelle asked Miss Williams if she could take a photo. Miss Williams said she didn't want her to. Michelle then said, "You've got to." Miss Williams asked who it was for. Michelle said she couldn't tell her … but then she did tell her.

"Did she laugh?"

"No. She smiled."

"What like?"

"A sort of kind smile, like she usually does."

"Did she say anything?"

"I don't think so. I wasn't really paying attention."

I then went across to Mrs. Addison's form room. I asked her if I could take her photo. She said, "Oh alright. Why do you want one of me?"

"I want to remember you. Smile how you usually do."

"How's that?"

"The way you smiled when you told me my German result."

Kate made sarcastic noises.

Didn't see Miss Williams all day. That hasn't happened for ages. I hope she's alright.

Friday 27th May 1988, Home

Was just about to take my camera to the last French lesson when Michelle took it off me. She said, "Don't you want another photo of Miss Williams?"—Bit strange?

At the end of the French lesson, Mr. McKay asked, "Who wants to do the last bit of French ever?" I said, "Me. I do."

Il disparut dans la foule (He disappeared into the crowd).

Ten minutes before break, Michelle came back.

"Did she mind?"

"No."

"What did she say?"

"Not another one?!"

At lunchtime I was coming downstairs in the sixth form block. Miss Williams was leaving the staff room (Friday is her half-day). She had a pair of jeans on. She looked up and saw me.

She said, "Natasha, what do you want with all these photos?"

I hesitated. "... I want to stick them on my wall at university."

She hesitated. "... To throw darts at?"

I looked her in the eyes and said, "No. ... You don't mind, do you?"

"I didn't have much choice. Michelle said 'You have to.' ... No. I don't mind."

"Thank you."

"That's alright. Bye."

"Bye."

My heart was beating like crazy. Her eyes!

Sunday 29th May 1988, Home

Started designing a large Miss Williams picture. Louise came round. Told her to get out of my bedroom.

Thursday 2nd June 1988, Home

Things always feel different when I've spoken to Miss Williams. It's so nice ... but then things go back to how they were.

Saw on the Upper Sixth notice board a 'good luck' card from Miss Williams to her German and French for Business people. Felt as hurt as I did during the O Levels, and this time she didn't even include the whole year. It really upsets me.

I was with Kate in the corridor when Imogen came up and asked me if I was talking to her again yet. Kate inquired. Imogen said because she fell asleep in Miss Williams's lesson. Kate laughed a lot.

Tuesday 7th June 1988, Home

When I got home my photos were there. I was so happy. They are brilliant. The second one of Miss Williams gave me a heart attack when I saw it.

Thursday 9th June 1988, Home

Latin set book exam. Enjoyed it. But the French literature exam was so tedious I just wanted to get up and walk out. I wrote such a load of rubbish I'll be lucky if I get 3%.

This evening Mum and Dad went out to an Anglo-French boat trip and meal. Before they went we were talking about my exams in the kitchen. I was thinking, "How can I get them to ask to see my photos?" ... I said to Mum, "Are you going to take your camera tonight?" It worked. They asked to see my photos. Mum looked at each one and passed it to Dad. When she came to the first one of Miss Williams, she looked at it and said, "Now, who's that?"

I thought, 'She knows perfectly well who it is.'

She said it must be a maths teacher because of the marks on the blackboard behind her.

Dad said, "It's Miss Williams." He's always so tactless.

Mum carried on going through them without mentioning the other one of Miss Williams. But she certainly didn't ask any questions. Great, eh?

Friday 10th June 1988, Home

Mum went out for the day, so Dad took me to get haggis and chips. I waited in the car with the passenger seat wound down, my feet up on the dashboard, looking at my two photos of Miss Williams. Dad came back from behind the car, so I didn't see him. ... I think he caught me looking at the photos. I hope so.

Saturday 11th June 1988, Home
Mum was shouting because there was too much food in the house, and because she didn't like the sofa and chairs that had come back this morning from being reupholstered.

Louise came round. She told me she'd given up her course at college, but Mum and Dad didn't know.

Showed Louise my photos of Miss Williams. She said, "Aww. She always looks so sweet."

Sunday 12th June 1988, Home
Eventually, after thirty-nine and a half hours, I finished my large Miss Williams design.

Tuesday 14th June 1988, Home
Didn't see Miss Williams today, but it never seems to matter like it used to, now that I have my photos.

Wednesday 15th June 1988, Home
Hair cut at last. The hairdressers has been changed around. I wish people would leave things the way they are.

Thursday 16th June 1988, Home

Phoned Truprint to ask about photo posters. Any discount for a hundred copies of a photo? (only ten percent)

Friday 17th June 1988, Home

Kate had left me a letter in the form room. It said, "I love you loads and I'll miss you something chronic." I wanted to cry.

Louise came round. She told me her leather jacket had been nicked at a party and she was claiming £140 off the insurance. She invited me to her and Nigel's barbecue tomorrow.

Saturday 18th June 1988, Home

Went down to the Centre. Bought *There's More to Love than Boy meets Girl* by The Communards. Fell in love with it yesterday evening whilst cherishing the second photo of Miss Williams.

Sent off the negative to Truprint and a cheque for five pounds for twenty reprints.

Sat on the stairs at Louise and Nigel's party and finished revising my Latin.

Gregory Harvey came. He looked just the same as at junior school ... but taller.

We went out into the garden and had a long chat about memories of infant and junior school. It was a lovely night. Drank Cherryade, Pomagne, and lager. Felt a bit dizzy, but it must have been with happiness, I didn't drink that much.

I miss Kate.

Gregory said that at school he thought I would reach degree standard, that I was always top of the class. He said he thought I was a girl to respect.

At home I taped The Communards record eight times in a row and cried about leaving school.

Sunday 19th June 1988, Home
Wrote a five page letter to Kate.

Tuesday 21st June 1988, Home
Went to Louise's, hoping to go on her sunbed. Nigel hadn't gone to work. He, his friend Nick, and Louise were watching tedious Bruce Lee videos. Nick had tattoos all over his arms.

A day or so ago it occurred to me that I should get a 'Miss Williams' tattoo on my left wrist—on the under-side, between my palm and my watch. I'd wanted one for ages, but I'd never thought where. I asked Nick if it hurt. He said it did, that the outline kills, but the shading doesn't because it's become numb by that time.

I said, "Does it hurt *here*?" (showing the place where I wanted it)

He said, "That's one of the most painful places."

Annoying. It's because the skin is so tight there, I think.

Wednesday 22nd June 1988, Home
To London with Mum on the train. I went off to Carnaby Street, she to Liberties. Saw a sign saying, 'T-shirt printing while you wait' for

£5.99. I went away … thought about it … went back again. The bloke told me to write on a piece of card what I wanted printing.

"Who is Miss Williams?"

"… Just someone I know."

Dad picked us up at the station. Mum and Dad had had the stairs carpet changed while we were out, without telling me. I could not believe it. "Why can't you just leave things alone?" I stormed off up to my bedroom and played *Heatseeker* by ACDC really loudly. Dad came up. I told him to go away.

9:50pm Mum came into my room uninvited. I said I had enough changes to cope with already and I hadn't kicked up a fuss about the chairs or the sofa or about their painting the piano a different colour, and I suppose tomorrow I'll find something different, and the next day?

Thursday 23rd June 1988, Home

Started sunbathing before 11am through till 6pm. I was just wearing my bra and knickers. The top of my chest and stomach are dead red and slightly painful. I love sunburn. It feels really nice.

Friday 24th June 1988, Home

Spent all day in town looking for something nice to wear to the leavers' cheese and wine evening. Wrote my first cheque for a shop. They asked me for my card. How am I supposed to know about things like that? They said they'd save the dress for me till Wednesday.

Saturday 25th June 1988, Home

We were eating lunch when Louise let herself in with her key, poked her head round the kitchen door in tears and said, "Mum, can I talk to you?" They went off upstairs.

Louise told Mum that she and Nigel kept having arguments. I'm not really sure what happened. She went back to Nigel's to pack her stuff. Then Dad picked her up.

Sunday 26th June 1988, Home

Put the finishing touches to my Miss Williams picture. About forty hours now.

Louise asked me if Miss Williams had a boyfriend.

I said, "I don't know."

She said, "I can't imagine Miss Williams giving anyone a passionate kiss, can you?"

I told her to shut up.

Monday 27th June 1988, Home

My last A Level today!

Just before the first lesson I went to the staff room to see Mr. McKay. Miss Williams appeared. I was really worried in case the yearbook had come out. It must have done. I couldn't look at her. She was wearing an apricot skirt and jumper.

... The yearbook is not out yet.

Opened the door for Miss Williams later. She walked through, smiling a lot, and said, "Thank you, Natasha" exactly like she used to. I grinned back a lot. I was so happy, I couldn't stop grinning all the way to my exam. Nobody else could ever affect me like that.

Louise told me that Gregory has invited me to his eighteenth birthday party at Millionaires on Friday. That's really touching. But *that* day? ...

Started my *Teach Yourself Russian* book.

Tuesday 28th June 1988, Home

Mum burst into my room 10:45am, said Miss Gordon was on the phone. I was asleep and confused.

Went to the phone. Miss Gordon said I should have taken my Latin books back to school yesterday and that Mr. McKay had taken everything out of my locker to look for them.

I thought, 'Oh no! ...' I had things in there with Miss Williams's name written on them, and a card for her, and designs of the French teachers' names. I could hardly speak. ...

Miss Gordon said, "Some of the things he found were very interesting. ... I don't think I'd better go on."

Wednesday 29th June 1988, Home

Phoned Truprint. They said my reprints wouldn't arrive until about 11th July. So annoyed.

Mum and Dad and I arrived at the leavers' cheese and wine evening at 7pm. Ten minutes later I suddenly looked up and there was Miss Williams. I blushed—and it didn't go away ALL NIGHT. I dread that happening. She was wearing a white skirt and white flowery blouse with padded shoulders and half-sleeves. She was talking to Liz. I hate that.

I was talking to Miss Gordon. She is leaving school. I asked her if she was sad and said, "You never show your feelings. You should."

She smiled knowingly. She said to me, "You're very unpredictable for some reason."

I said, "That's a really nice thing to say."

"You are."

"If you say so."

"I do."

Took a photo of Mrs. Addison while she wasn't looking. She turned round and laughed and said to Mum and Dad, "It's like being on *Candid Camera*."

I was standing near the door at the back of the hall, talking to Miss Byron about our going to Russia, when Miss Williams walked out about 8:30pm. I didn't realise that she was leaving for good. I was really upset. I hardly had any chance to look at her because I kept going outside where it was cooler to try and get rid of my red cheeks.

I just want to be with her.

Thursday 30th June 1988, Home

Went into school. I was the only one from the Upper Sixth there.

11:25am went up to Mrs. Harrison's art room with my design of Miss Williams's name. I asked her, "Could you put up a picture for me?"

"If it's good enough?"

I showed it to her.

She said, "Miss Williams. Do you like her?"

I nodded, "Yes."

She asked me why I didn't give it to her instead.

"She wouldn't want it."

"I'm sure she would. She could put it in her new form room." (the needlework room).

Mrs. Harrison said she'd put it up next year. I asked her not to tell Miss Williams.

The school magazine came out today. They had picked one of my designs as the cover. I'd had no idea. Thrilled.

Friday 1st July 1988, Home

Came to school at the usual time. Begged Claire to come to prize-giving assembly with me (as Miss Williams would be there). We were the only ones from the Upper Sixth. Miss Williams sat behind us.

Final assembly was in the afternoon. As we waited for Miss Byron to arrive, my eyes began to fill up. Then tears were streaming down my face. I had been really worried that I wouldn't be able to cry. I would never have forgiven myself.

No more assembly ever again. And we sang the School Song for the last time.

Walked down the corridor for the last time. Cried more than before.

Stood outside the staff room. A group of younger girls were waiting for Miss Williams. She came out and said sweetly, "What do you Henriettas want?" I hadn't heard her call anyone that for ages.

When she spoke to one of the girls she kissed her on the cheek. You can guess how I felt. I both died with jealousy and thought it was lovely at the same time.

She turned to go back into the staff room. And I said, "Miss Williams?"

She turned round.

I asked her, "Can I take a photo of you, please?"

She replied that Michelle had taken some, and she asked, "Have you got them?"

I said I had.

Mr. Gilbert turned up. Miss Williams said, "Take one of us together."

I said firmly and quite loudly, "No."

Mr. Gilbert confirmed, "That was definitely a 'no.'"

So, I took a photo of Miss Williams.

And then I took another one.

At this point she said, "This is the last one." And she insisted on it being with someone else. She even went back into the staff room to find someone. She came back without anyone. Miss Halsie was approaching the staff room. So, I said I would photograph the two of them together. Miss Halsie said she'd just get out of her coat, and she went into the staff room.

While waiting, Miss Williams looked away. I took a third photograph of her. She looked a bit surprised. I explained to her that I hadn't got one of her profile.

Miss Halsie didn't re-emerge, so I got some other teachers together and took a fourth photo.

Then they all just walked off towards the assembly hall. And I took a photo of Miss Williams's back.

Went to see Miss Williams's new form room (the needlework room). I suddenly had the idea to write something with drawing pins on her notice board. I had to collect more drawing pins from other form rooms. I wrote out:

MISS WILLIAMS

I LOVE YOU

I wanted to add 'NATASHA' at the bottom, but ran out of drawing pins. This took me from 12:30pm till after 1pm. Really felt like a burglar. Thought I might get locked in, or that the cleaners might come, or that *she* might. ...

As I went out of the doors at the end of the corridor leading to the needlework room, about to go downstairs, I saw Miss Williams's white handbag and the edge of her dress. I could hear her and Mr. Gilbert's voices.

I took off my shoes ready to dash off upstairs if necessary. But she went off in another direction, calling back to Mr. Gilbert an extremely un-Miss-Williams thing: "If you can't be good, be careful."

I waited until I felt it was safe, then made my escape.

Sat on the window sill in the sixth form block till 4:20pm when a bloke came to lock up.

Went to visit Sara, told her I'd taken loads of photos of Miss Williams.

Sara said, "Oh, you don't still fancy *her*, do you?" and she bought me a chocolate chip ice-cream.

Got back 6:40pm. I wanted to stay at home this evening and be sad, but Louise persuaded me to come out for Gregory's birthday. I wore my white dress.

Gregory, his friend Gary, Louise, Nigel, and I went for pizza, then to The Lion. Drank snakebite and black. Then to Millionaires. The boys bought us loads of drinks.

Nigel wanted to talk to me privately. We moved to another table. He told me that Louise is pregnant. I was thrilled. She'd told Mum the day she came home, but Mum wouldn't let her tell me because of my A Levels and leaving school. Louise didn't want to tell me herself. She didn't know how.

By the end of the evening I was pretty drunk. I fell over on the floor of the nightclub. Nigel and Gary (who has lovely eyes) had to carry me to the taxi outside.

I was hugging Gary, saying, "I don't want to leave" (meaning school). In the taxi I lay on Louise's lap. I kept repeating myself ...

"I love her. ... I love Miss Williams and she hates me. ... Lower Seventh, Upper Seventh, Lower Eighth. ... Will you tell her that I love her? ..."

ETC.

We got home at 12:45am. Dad came to the door and was a bit cross. Louise took me upstairs to her room, undressed me, and put me on her bed. She switched the light out. I said I was going to be sick. A bit went on her bed and carpet, and the rest in a carrier bag. She took me into my room.

(It was the girl's right cheek.)

Saturday 2nd July 1988, Home

Woke up towards 8:30am. Felt tired and dizzy. Got up towards 11am. My Miss Williams reprints had arrived.

Walked to the library at the Centre. Slowly. Felt sick. Asked for a map of Miss Williams's town. The librarian could only find a really simple one in a book, so I couldn't work out where Miss Williams might live. Looked in the telephone directory for where Miss Williams once told us her parents live. If only I had a clue about her family.

Walked home. Sat in the living room. I asked Louise to get me an Aspirin. Mum was angry, said I was "stupid and disgusting."

Women's Wimbledon final. Martina v. Steffi Graff. POO, Martina lost. I think she's great.

Louise went to the Boat House to work and I cleaned my sick up.

Sunday 3rd July 1988, Home

10:05pm phone call from Gregory's friend Gary. He was with Louise and Nigel. He kept asking me when I was free. Then Nigel was on the phone. He said Louise and I were to come round to his house tomorrow night—to cheer up Gary.

Louise told me later that Gary had been really nervous about phoning me, he thought I wouldn't want to speak to him. She said he was in love with me, and that he wants a photo of me.

Monday 4th July 1988, Home

8:50pm Dad rather unwillingly drove Louise and me round to Nigel's.

Louise, Nigel, Gary, and I sat in Nigel's bedroom and talked for about an hour. Gary and I were sitting together on the sofa. Bit awkward. Louise and Nigel kept kissing and arguing.

We all went down to the pub at the Centre. Gary bought everything. I had a Coke and crisps. We talked about murderers and prison (Well, *I* did). We went back for some of Louise's stuff to bring home.

Dad came at 10:45pm. Gary helped carry some of Louise's stuff back to the car. Dad was in an odd mood. Louise went back into the house, leaving me talking with Gary by the car. I said I'd better get in the car because Dad was in a mood. He said, "Have a nice holiday," and tapped me on the right shoulder.

In the car Dad said I was stupid for going round there.

"What do you mean?"

"Do I have to spell it out for you? ... Hasn't she told you?"

Presumably he meant the baby. Dad's being really strange towards Louise.

Learnt some Russian.

Tuesday 5th July 1988, Home

Louise working at the Boat House. She blacked out and fainted.

Nigel rang Louise from the phone box at the Centre. Gary was with him. He asked to speak to me. We talked for about five minutes. It's a bit embarrassing.

It occurred to me this afternoon that Miss Williams's parents are not in the telephone directory because ... the funeral she attended in the Lower Fifths?

Wednesday 6th July 1988, Home

Asked in Boots about things they could make out of photos, like place mats, beer mats. Went to the library. Looked up 'Williams' in every single telephone directory. It took hours. Brilliant. I always wanted to be a detective.

Thursday 7th July 1988, Home

Went down to the library. Ordered three books on Sapphic poetry! Very interesting (I hope). Learnt some more Russian while I was there.

When Louise came back from the Boat House, she told me that I could work there. I'm to go with her next time. I've never had a proper job.

Nigel got his job in Sainsbury's.

Friday 8th July 1988, Home

Louise came home after a morning interview, having argued with Nigel. She was crying loads. Nigel had bought a Top Man card and is getting into debt. He told her to get out and take her baby with her.

Saturday 9th July 1988, Home > Russia

Our hotel has six thousand rooms. It took Louise and me a long time to find ours again.

Sunday 10th July 1988, Russia

Morning coach tour round Moscow. Afternoon Lenin Museum.

At dinner Louise was being rude to Mum, and Mum was getting in a real mood. She kept threatening to leave the restaurant and go home.

Dad came up to our room and really shouted at Louise, more than I've ever heard before—shaking his fists. He came back later to apologise.

Monday 11th July 1988, Russia

Mum and Dad and Louise went out. I stayed, lay on the bed, listened to my Walkman, and adored my photo of Miss Williams.

10pm went to see the changing of the guard outside Lenin's tomb.

Tuesday 12th July 1988, Russia

Moscow State Circus. Spectacular.

Wednesday 13th July 1988, Russia

Round the Kremlin in the morning.

Train to Leningrad. Incredibly hot. Louise and I were talking about one of her friends and whether she was gay. Louise was saying the most incredible things. I'd had absolutely no idea. When Louise was fifteen she was so scared that she might be a lesbian. She really liked one of the girls in the shoe shop where she had her Saturday job, thought she was really pretty, and was so sad when the girl got engaged. And if the girl didn't turn up to work one Saturday, Louise had a miserable time. She was so scared that she fancied her. Amazing.

Thursday 14th July 1988, Russia

I went down to breakfast ten minutes late. Dad had gone to look for me. Mum was really angry with me.

Coach tour round the city. I was crying.

Back to the hotel for lunch. I couldn't find the hotel card to lock our room with, so I was late again. Mum shouted at me "It's not good enough." I was thinking about this, and then about leaving school and where I sit on the window sill in the sixth form block and watch Miss Williams going from the staff room to lessons—the way her skirt waves when she walks and the way she leans over to one side when she carries her tape recorder. I cried and I couldn't stop. It is thoroughly impossible for me to understand that I have left school. Mum stopped being nasty to me then, but she didn't stop her stupid complaining.

Friday 15th July 1988, Russia

Tour round the Summer Palace. Louise felt dizzy again, so we all left the group and went out into the gardens. I have forty-six mosquito bites.

Sunday 17th July 1988, Russia > Home

Tour round the Leningrad cathedrals in the morning. Went round with Andy Wiseman, a producer at the BBC. I said what a tedious job it must have been to produce that amount of artistic detail. Andy pointed out that it might well have been the most thrilling event in the artists' lives to contribute to such a beautiful project. I liked that.

I asked the guide some questions. She thinks our Queen is a decoration: old-fashioned, but nice. Her favourite Soviet leader is Lenin because he's modest, intelligent, and good. She has lost respect for Gorbachev because he bought diamonds for his wife. He couldn't afford this with his own money, so he used state money.

I told her I didn't think Russians were allowed to express an opinion. She replied that she thinks these stories she hears about Russia from foreigners are really funny—that the Russians eat babies, and take children away from their parents to indoctrinate them into The Party.

We got home from holiday 8:10pm. Louise got some rejection letters from companies, and a really sweet card from Nigel. It said he loved her and that he, she, and the baby could be together and love each other forever. He wanted Louise to go round to see him. Dad took her.

My photos had arrived. I was so nervous I couldn't open them. I unpacked. Two hours later I plucked up courage. I was dying with worry in case they hadn't come out.

Strange feeling when I did look at them. Mum would call it an "anti-climax." It seems the more photos I get of Miss Williams, the less I appreciate them. I love them though.

Monday 18th July 1988, Home

Went to the Job Centre with Louise. And we enquired in McDonald's about a job too. We filled in long forms and got interview times for tomorrow.

Nigel called round towards 7pm. Dad opened the door. Nigel asked him, "Is Louise there?" Dad said nothing, shut the door on him, and went and called Louise.

Tuesday 19th July 1988, Home

Bought *I Don't Want to Talk About It* by Everything But The Girl.

Louise went for her McDonald's interview. I went off to the library. Asked for *Annie on my Mind* by Nancy Garden. I heard about this book in the advice section in Just Seventeen magazine. They didn't have it. There were two other books mentioned in the advice section. Asked the librarian for *The Well of Loneliness* by Radclyffe Hall. It was on loan. She said it was a well-known book. I felt a bit embarrassed and silly because she knew what it was about. I was trying not to laugh. Tried to look serious, which made it worse. They did have *Patience and Sarah* by Isabel Miller. I was very happy.

Mum showed me her photos of Russia and I showed her my photos. When she saw the first picture, she just said, "Ah ... Miss Williams."

Louise got the McDonald's job.

Phoned up about a pre-packing factory job. Have to wait to be picked up by the petrol station at 6:45am tomorrow.

Wednesday 20th July 1988, Home

Got up 6am. A bloke in a car picked me up at the petrol station roundabout and took me to where a van was waiting. Long, bumpy ride. Got to the factory 8am. Was given an overall and a hat. Nothing was explained to me. I was just told to help with the onions. And the grapes.

In the quarter hour break I read *Patience and Sarah*.

At lunch I read *Patience and Sarah*, listening to *I Don't Want to Talk About It* by Everything But The Girl on my Walkman.

Cucumbers.

Lettuces.

Peppers.

Finished at 4pm. Ride home in the van was awful. Felt so ill.

Mum and Dad and I went out to an Anglo-French evening. I just wanted to get back to my book.

Thursday 21st July 1988, Home

I got a rejection letter from McDonald's. I was really angry. I have eleven O Levels! Why did I bother?

Event at the showground. An army chap, twenty-seven years old, told me I had beautiful eyes and asked me out to dinner. I said, "You're a bit old, aren't you?"

8:55pm Louise came back from Nigel's. She was angry with me. She said they'd had an argument because I'd asked Nigel why he'd knocked at the door the other day. And I'd told Nigel that Dad thought that he'd taken his daughter away from him, and that Dad thought too that Louise had left college because of the baby. I didn't think I'd said anything wrong. I was just discussing things with him. ... Sorry.

Friday 22nd July 1988, Home

Mum, Dad, and Louise all out this morning. And I woke up about 8am. Decided it was a good opportunity to ring round the Williams clan. Got a bit nervous. Kept putting it off. Had a shower and did a mile on Louise's exercise bike.

Eventually decided to go for it ... when Mum came home towards 11am to check that I'd got up for my driving lesson at 11:30am.

I planned the questions I would ask on the phone, on a piece of paper. But the silly woman wouldn't go back to work. How annoying.

Asked Dad to phone McDonald's and ask them what the problem was. They said it was only because I hadn't wanted to work Saturdays.

Finished reading *Patience and Sarah.* Re-read great chunks of it. And renewed it at the library. It's addictive and beautiful, especially page 128. *Love* that.

Went to McDonald's. Told them I could work Saturdays. I got the job. So happy that I went to Virgin's and bought *All Fired Up* by Pat Benetar.

Saturday 23rd July 1988, Home

Drew Kate's birthday card. Took four hours.

We all went out to a Caribbean evening. Louise kissed me on the left cheek and said, "Miss Williams will be jealous. ... You hope. ... Or does she already have a girlfriend?" I thought that was hilarious. I laughed a lot.

Monday 25th July 1988, Home

Louise and I out to work at McDonald's 10am. Started by dressing the burgers. Quite good fun. Then poured out drinks. Ajax-ed equipment at the front. Cooked French fries, then back on dressings and Ajax. Took my break at 3pm. Had nine chicken McNuggets, large fries with mild mustard and barbecue sauce, medium Coke, and chocolate donut. Felt ill.

Nigel came in and asked where Louise was. She had lied to him about her working there because he didn't want her to. His friend had seen her and told him. Nigel said he wouldn't see her again until she stopped, and wouldn't give her any more money for the baby.

I decided not to look at my Miss Williams photos for three weeks if possible. Locked them in the box Sharon gave me to hide our letters in.

Tuesday 26th July 1988, Home

McDonald's 10am. Not so interesting today. One of the girls was really ratty with me because I kept getting Ketchup everywhere.

Louise has at long last, and after about thirty interviews, got a job. With British Telecom. She is very happy.

Wednesday 27th July 1988, Home

Feels like I've been working at McDonald's for years.

Letter from Sharon. I loved her so much.

Louise was quite upset today. She went to see Nigel for the first time since he caught her in McDonald's. He told her they were finished. He knows she planned the pregnancy to get away from Mum and Dad.

Thursday 28th July 1988, Home

At McDonald's I was taking some rubbish up the stairs. I slipped and fell on the right side of my face. My nose was bleeding. It felt numb and bruised. My right cheek killed, my teeth felt like they were falling out. It really, really hurt. I was crying. They fetched me some ice in a cloth and said I could go and sit in the crew room.

John and John were in the crew room. We were talking about teaching because John asked me what I wanted to be. The conversation turned to Clause 28. John said teachers should be allowed to give an unbiased view of homosexuality because people think it's a disease. The other John said homosexuality is "demonic."

...

My thumb got burnt by a girl on grill passing a spatula over it. And Louise got a nasty burn on her arm cooking the fries.

8:25pm Kate rang from the Outer Hebrides to thank me for the birthday card. We only spoke for five minutes. Bit strange. It didn't really seem like she wanted to talk to me.

Friday 29th July 1988, Home

A card came from the library for one of the books I ordered: *Sappho of Lesbos—Her Life and Times*. Dad saw it. I hope he doesn't know anything about this. ... But then again, who cares?

Monday 1st August 1988, Home

Letter from Kate this morning. It was a lovely letter, and I had been so worried.

      When I got home, the school yearbook had arrived. I was so excited. Started at the beginning and read through to my page. Took about three hours.

Tuesday 2nd August 1988, Home

My first day off. Absolute beaut. A lie-in. Had the house to myself—just how I like it.

      3:20pm went to the library to get the Sappho book, and looked for some more lesbian (I love that word now) books. Didn't find any, but saw *The Catcher in The Rye*. Several months ago I watched a documentary that said Mark Chapman murdered John Lennon because he'd read that book. Got it out.

Wednesday 3rd August 1988, Home

Went to the library and ordered *Annie On My Mind* by Nancy Garden, and looked for *The Well of Loneliness*.

Saturday 6th August 1988, Home

Argument with Mum about her always asking me when I'm working. *Really* annoys me.

McDonald's shift 5pm till close. One of the boys said to me, "You have a very pleasant face. You're always smiling." Another boy then said I had ten out of ten.

Ten out of ten? What for?

About 1am Dad phoned McDonald's to ask when and how I would be getting home. I was really mad about that. They told him that I'd finish about 2:30am and get a taxi.

We finished 2:05am and one by one we sat in the sink in the back room while the others hosed us down. It was so funny. We were drenched. We clocked off 2:15am.

I asked the taxi driver to drop me off at the end of our road, just by the path into the woods, 2:45am.

Spent two hours lying on the grass under a lamppost, reading *The Catcher in The Rye*.

Decided to go for a walk down to the Centre. Sat on a bench down there and read for ten minutes ... then got a bit nervous as there were no houses nearby.

Coming back 5:08am I noticed it had got light. I was walking up our road when Dad and Louise pulled up in the car.

Oh dear. ... I got in.

"Where do you think you've been?" Etc.

Dad said they'd got the police out. I was a missing person. I couldn't believe it. Well, I suppose I could.

There was a policeman sitting at the kitchen table. Louise went off to bed.

The policeman wanted to know what I was doing, and warned me of dangers. This was interspersed with cold, sarcastic remarks from Mum and Dad.

The policeman left. Mum and Dad started shouting. I said forcefully that if you love someone you don't shout at them. They were quite nice then. I knew that would work.

We sat in the kitchen and had long discussions about what love was. Mum said there was no such thing as a perfect friend. I said there was (meaning Miss Williams). I said I knew one, and I started crying.

Mum hugged me and asked if it was Sharon? No. Kate? No. I said I didn't want to talk about it. I wonder what they thought?

Monday 8th August 1988, Home

Nigel got a free dog called Tizer.

Started *1984* by George Orwell.

Today—very lucky day—8th of the 8th 1988. And at 8:18pm, Fergie had her first baby, a little girl.

Tuesday 9th August 1988, Home

A drag. The worst day. Drinks pulling, Ajax-ing, dressing the burgers. "Where did you get to Saturday night?"

"How did you know?"

"Everybody knows."

Oh great.

Thursday 11th August 1988, Home

Awake till 5:30am, crying and listening to my Walkman. I was thinking all about school through the years. It's killing me. Don't ever forget how much you love that place. I'm so afraid I'm going to forget.

Friday 12th August 1988, Home

My favourite sort of day: I'm at home, and everybody else isn't.

Got my list of Williams phone numbers and rang the nurse— because nurses are nice. No answer. Rang the first name on my list. Put the phone down after two or three rings. Rang the nurse again. No answer. My heart was beating so fast. Rang the next number. Answer machine. And the next. No reply.

Phoned the town hall to see if there was any way of tracing a person's relatives. I was told not.

Had a gorgeous bubble bath for nearly an hour. Serenaded an imaginary Miss Williams. Sang her *The Power of Love* by Frankie Goes To Hollywood. I want her.

Saturday 13th August 1988, Home

McDonald's pay us fortnightly. Got very first pay slip ever: £137.68.

Met people outside McDonald's 7pm. Went to The Warwick for one of the managers' leaving party. Had Coke, bitter lemon, orange juice, Appletiser—all bought for me by boys.

They were saying something about Wednesday nights at The Warwick. I inquired. They told me that Wednesday is Gay Night.

How fascinating. They were laughing about it. "Don't bend over." (ha)

I love wearing foundation. I don't go red at all. It's absolutely brilliant.

Sunday 14th August 1988, Home

Nigel rang midday to tell Louise that Diana, her budgie, had died. The cats had got it again, and it was bleeding.

Louise saw the yearbook and read my section. She read 'What or who will you miss most?' where I'd answered 'Miss Williams.' She said, "You can't put that in here. She'll think you're really strange." I thought that was funny.

Monday 15th August 1988, Home

During break, Anita from school, who also works at McDonald's said, "You've got a strange idea of what you're going to miss most." I didn't catch on at the time. I thought she was on about the 'Good memories' section. I asked her how she remembered my answer out of all the other people's answers in there. She said it was because mine was so strange.

Tuesday 16th August 1988, Home

Saw two of the Lower Fourths in McDonald's. Asked if they were doing German next year to get the conversation round to Miss Williams. They were laughing at her clothes. One of them said, "She could get a husband if she changed herself."

The new girl burnt herself on the grill and Darren Grace was laughing.

I said, "Aren't boys heartless."

Darren said, "I'm sure you're a lesbian—the things you say about men."

I didn't reply, just walked out. I couldn't stop laughing. I thought it was hilarious.

Bought an extra fair concealer stick in Boots. Feel really confident with foundation on.

Wednesday 17th August 1988, Home

This evening I walked round and round outside for twenty-five minutes listening to *Look Out Any Window* by Bruce Hornsby and The Range.

Thursday 18th August 1988, Home

Got to the sixth form block 2:07pm. I asked for my results slip to be put in an envelope because I didn't want to see it. Sat in the common room, listening to other people's results, fiddling nervously with my envelope.

Miss Byron walked in and said to me, "Yours were good, weren't they."

I replied, "Don't tell me!" (to Miss Byron!)

I went down to a classroom by myself and opened the envelope. When my Latin result sank in I screamed and punched the locker behind me. Grade A.

Bit disappointed with a grade C for Spanish, but too happy about the Latin to care.

We hung around the sixth form block, waiting to see if the Oxford results would come in the second post. They didn't.

Went to look at my drawing pin message for Miss Williams. At the bottom of the stairs was a 'No entry' sign because of cleaning. I hesitated ... but went up anyway. The door was locked. Tried to look through the window. I think the drawing pins been taken out. How annoying.

Phoned Mum 3:50pm. She went berserk with my Latin result. Dad had been phoning her every ten minutes. And Louise had rung twice! Rang Louise. She was surprisingly delighted and told everyone in her office.

Friday 19th August 1988, Home

Letter from UCCA accepting me ... for Miss Williams's old university.

5:30pm Mum drove me to school. Asked one of the teachers to fold my French result slip before giving it to me. Went to the Upper Fourth garden. Covered the slip of paper with the envelope ... and slowly moved it down. ...

"Shit."

Felt disappointed, helpless, upset.

Went back to the sixth form block. Mrs. Addison smiled and said to me, "Don't you dare tell me you're not pleased."

I said that I wasn't pleased with a grade B and that I would retake it next year.

"Don't you dare."

Miss Byron asked me, "Are you pleased?"

I replied, "… Nearly."

Gave Mum the thumbs-down.

Dad asked, "How did you do?"

"Crap."

We went out to dinner to "celebrate." Ha ha. Sulked the whole time.

Saturday 20th August 1988, Home

Extremely upset last night. Tantrums like a little baby. Same this morning.

Sunday 21st August 1988, Home

Drew 'Thank you' cards for the Latin teachers.

Monday 22nd August 1988, Home

Mum in a real mood about cleaning the house for the French.

In the afternoon went downstairs. Mum was in the kitchen, crying. She said she didn't like everything changing: me going to university, Louise's baby, my results, and now the French coming.

Pubs are now allowed to open 11am-11pm. Pity. I prefer tradition.

Thursday 25th August 1988, Home

Congratulations card from Miss Byron. It had the colours of the French flag on it and cost 60p. She can't have bought a card for everyone?

> Letter from Kate. Wrote twelve sides back to her.
>
> I want Miss Williams. I yearn for her eyes.

Saturday 27th August 1988, Home

Got home from work 7:25pm. I'd forgotten my key. Went round to Nigel's to borrow Louise's key. We sat around talking. Nigel told Louise to go. He started swearing and shouting really loudly at her. She was crying. He shouted more. He had wanted to go out secretly without her.

Sunday 28th August 1988, Home

At lunch Dad gave me a card from the library for *Annie On My Mind*. I was delighted. The card must have come yesterday. I wonder why I didn't see it?

Wednesday 31st August 1988, Home

Went to the town library. Got *Annie On My Mind*.

> The hairdressers hadn't got my name down, so I had to wait two hours. I didn't mind. I read. The girl who washed my hair asked me about having to wait. I said it was OK because I was reading.
>
> "What were you reading?" (I hadn't expected that. ...)
>
> "... A book."

"Really? Does this book have a title?"

"Yes."

"I'll say no more."

All the time she was washing my hair I wanted to burst out laughing, wondering what she must be thinking.

Finished the whole book today. Disappointing, considering the excellent title.

Thursday 1st September 1988, Home

It's sad how nobody says "Pinch punch ..." anymore. I'm too old.

Monday 5th September 1988, Home

Rang Emily. Asked her about the first day back at school, and asked her to send me all the forms for school plays, events, etc. She promised she would.

I looked in the telephone directory for Mrs. Harrison's number, but there were so many of them that I decided to wait till Wednesday and call the staff room at break. Emily didn't mention my Miss Williams picture, and surely she would have done if Mrs. Harrison had put it up yet?

I wonder if Miss Williams has seen the yearbook or has been told about the drawing pin message I left her? I want to go back to school.

Prisoner Cell Block H on tonight 12:15am. The portable is still at the menders, so I asked Dad if I could watch it downstairs. He kept shouting "No" at me over and over for ages. I got really angry and shouted at him, "I'm never going to forget this."

Tuesday 6th September 1988, Home

Last day at McDonald's. Tedious.

10:30am Nigel and Louise were in court versus their landlord for not paying rent, not keeping the house tidy, and refusing to get out. They were fined £200 and given four weeks to leave.

When I got home I found the TV on my dressing table. Dad must have left work early to go and fetch it. So sweet—just the sort of thing he would do.

Wednesday 7th September 1988, Home

11:40am, alone in the house, I phoned the staff room. Asked to speak to Mrs. Harrison. She wasn't there. I was pretty relieved as I was so nervous. Tried again at 11:48am. Someone went off to have a look. While I was waiting, the school bell rang. Felt very sad. Mrs. Gatwick came to the phone and asked in her usual grumpy tone (which didn't help my nerves) if she could take a message because Mrs. Harrison was tied up. I replied that I wanted to speak to her personally. She asked if I'd like her to phone me at lunch and she took my number.

Mrs. Harrison didn't phone. At 3:55pm I rang the staff room again. One of the teachers asked who it was so that she could tell Mrs. Harrison.

4:03pm I rang again. A secretary said she'd put a message in Mrs. Harrison's pigeonhole as I'd been trying all day.

Thursday 8th September 1988, Home

Failed my second driving test.

Wrote a poem to Miss Williams.

Friday 9th September 1988, Home

Went to a party at The Scotgate 8pm. Drank Coke and orange juice. When I got home, I realised I'd forgotten to ask people if they'd had a congratulations card from Miss Byron. How annoying.

Saturday 10th September 1988, Home

Louise phoned and told Mum and Dad that she'd just got engaged. They were really happy. They hadn't known that she was already engaged. I don't want Louise to get married. It makes me feel inferior. But I'm happy for her really.

Sewed bottoms of black jeans to make them thinner.

Sunday 11th September 1988, Home

Mum and Dad and I went to the Horse Trials. Saw Cass. Asked her if she got a card from Miss Byron. She said that Miss Byron had phoned up, but that she wasn't in. Saw Philippa. She didn't get a phone call.

Monday 12th September 1988, Home

Waited for Mrs. Harrison to ring this morning. She didn't.

Went into town. In M&S saw Claire on the till. Had to buy a bag of crisps to get to talk to her. She did get a card. She got a phone call as well.

Bumped into Ellen. She got into uni even without the right grades. She didn't get a card or a phone call.

Rang the staff room at 3:53pm. Was told they were in assembly. Rang at 4pm and someone said she would put a note in Mrs. Harrison's pigeonhole to ring me.

Wednesday 14th September 1988, Home

1:23pm phoned the staff room. Mrs. Harrison wasn't there.

Thursday 15th September 1988, Home

Took *Annie On My Mind* back, and got out *Fear of Flying* by Erica Jong. Saw Anita in the library. She got a card from Miss Byron.

Friday 16th September 1988, Home

Louise bought me an extra fair concealer stick.

Caught the bus to school. Got there 9:50am. Looked for my Miss Williams picture. It wasn't anywhere. Went into Miss Williams's form room. There's a large calendar hanging over where I wrote my drawing pin message. It doesn't cover all the holes. You can still see some of the message on the left-hand side.

Went to find Mrs. Harrison. Miss Tennyson told me that the art teachers were on a trip. Rats.

Hid in the main cloakroom 10:20am to watch the teachers walk past at break. Saw Mrs. Duffield and Mrs. Rodd through the window.

Went to room 19, where Miss Williams would be. From the corridor, I saw her head by the blackboard. *Love.*

Went to the staff room. Asked for Mrs. Addison, Mr. McKay, Mrs. Duffield. None of them were there. Asked when Prize Day would be. It's 25th November.

Hid in the cloakroom again. Saw Miss Williams walking to the staff room at break. She was wearing a great jacket. She has had her hair trimmed.

Met Emily. We went to the cookery rooms for two lessons to make fruit salad. Felt very sad.

In the afternoon I sat in my usual spot on the window sill in the sixth form block. Saw Miss Williams come out of the staff room. She was wearing her navy blue and yellow dress.

Back to the staff room to see Mrs. Addison. Asked her to take some photos of Miss Williams for me. She said no.

Before the end of school, I went to the top of the stairs towards the needlework room. I watched the door. A little after the bell, Miss Williams came out and went downstairs. I really felt like following her.

4:10pm I sat in my spot on the window sill again, desperately wanting to see and speak to Miss Williams. I watched both exits from the staff room. Jumped out of my skin each time the sixth form block staff room exit opened. Sat there till 6:45pm, hoping.

Had the idea to put a love heart by Miss Williams's name on two notices of hers on the notice board outside the staff room. Did it.

Saturday 17th September 1988, Home

Wrote to Mr. McKay. Sent him a stamped addressed envelope for the school events calendar and diary.

Got passport photos done in the photo booth in Boots, for university halls of residence. Ugly!

Monday 19th September 1988, Home

Went down to the Centre. Got passport photos done again in the photo booth.

Tuesday 20th September 1988, Home

In Boots my eyes drifted onto the CDs. There was one by a Christina Ortiz, a French classical pianist. She is about the most beautiful woman I have ever seen.

Wednesday 21st September 1988, Home

Sent off to Truprint for a large photo poster (£8.95) and a medium-sized photo poster (£4.95) of Miss Williams.

Thursday 22nd September 1988, Home

Rang the Boat House 11:15am. I've got another job! Have to be there at 9:30am tomorrow to polish silver.

Sharon phoned 1:40pm. We talked for twenty or thirty minutes. It's like she's a stranger now. Bit sad, eh?

Went to WHSmith. Looked for things by Christina Ortiz. Nothing.

Mum dropped me off at the Centre. Got some passport photos done.

Tonight Louise came into my room with an envelope from Mum's parents. It had a Surrey post mark on it. Mum had asked her who it was from as she recognised the handwriting. Louise was shaking. She'd told Mum it was from an estate agent. Mum had said sarcastically that she didn't think they could afford a house in Surrey.

Friday 23rd September 1988, Home
Michelle and I went on a pub crawl this evening. I had bitter lemon, Appletiser, and Coke. She was drinking brandy and lemonade. We were singing the School Song loudly in the street. Felt really sad.

Saturday 24th September 1988, Home
Polished crockery and glasses at the Boat House. Discussing the Bible and hell with a Roman Catholic and a couple of Mormons made the time fly.

During lunch they were talking about how awful Edwina Currie is. The Roman Catholic called her "ugly." I said, "I think she's attractive, actually." He called me "Lezzie."

Have filled my second book of Green Shield stamps.

Read *Mastering German* to chapter seven.

Monday 26th September 1988, Home

Mr. McKay sent me a school calendar and diary, and wrote me a nice letter as well.

My last *Prisoner Cell Block H* at home. ...

Tuesday 27th September 1988, Home

Mum took me to Sainsbury's to buy me tuck for university.

Fourth lot of passport photos from the photo booth. Still ugly.

Went to the library. Photocopied twenty-four pages of this school diary in case I lose it (£2.40. Bargain).

Wednesday 28th September 1988, Home

Got two more lots of passport photos done. Awful.

Returned Erica Jong book to the library without reading most of it. Sat in the library and read the lesbian chapter of her book *How To Save Your Own Life*.

Got Philips Ladyshave from Green Shield Stamps shop.

To Boots for stationery for uni. Went and looked at Christina Ortiz again.

Friday 30th September 1988, Home

Got to school 11:46am. Waited in the main cloakroom till the end of break. Saw Miss Williams's head as she left the staff room. When safe, I went to the cloakroom in the sixth form block to leave my coat.

Saw Miss Williams three times in the lunch hour from my spot on the window sill in the sixth form block.

Off to see if my Miss Williams picture was up yet. No! Went to find Mrs. Harrison in the junior art room. She took me outside. I asked her if she'd changed her mind about putting it up. She said she'd been ill, had been busy, had had conferences, but *would* put it up. She had told Miss Williams that she could have it in her room after a few weeks. I had asked her not to mention it to Miss Williams!

"What did you tell Miss Williams?"

"That you've done a picture with her name worked into the design."

"What did she say?"

"She just looked really surprised."

"Has she seen it?"

"No."

"Did she ask to?"

"Yes. But I was in a hurry."

"When did you tell her this?"

"At the end of last term."

"Has she mentioned it this term?"

"No."

Exciting, eh?

Went into the Lower Sixth common room to ask if anyone was learning Italian. No.

3:18pm I went up to the school shop for the first time in years. Bought a school crest badge to sew on my clothes, and took a small and a large plastic bag with the school emblem on.

Saw Miss Williams coming back from her last lesson 3:32pm. She may have seen me.

3:38pm Miss Williams walked from her shelf to the staff room. She looked towards the window sill in the sixth form block. Was she checking to see if I was there? I think she saw me.

Sat waiting till 4:30pm to see Miss Williams again, although I knew she had left.

On the way to the bus station I saw one of my Latin teachers. I told her I was heartbroken about my French result and was planning to take it again. She said I mustn't, that I must concentrate on getting my degree, and on finding myself a man (!).

Told her I didn't want to get married.

She couldn't believe it. "Why?"

"I don't want to be tied to a man for the rest of my life."

She talked about it as if people who weren't married were second class citizens.

When I got home I felt really upset that I didn't go and talk to Miss Williams. It was my last chance. ... She was wearing a white blouse and bright blue skirt.

Saturday 1st October 1988, Home
Started packing. It's so sad.

Sunday 2nd October 1988, Home > University
Felt very, very sad when we left the house, 12:10pm. Mum and Dad and I got to The Halls (the halls of residence) 3:35pm. Judging by the slippers and dressing gown in the room already, my room mate

isn't too trendy. On returning with Dad and my luggage, my room mate was there. She's from Lebanon. Her name is Marie-Rose.

Mum and Dad and I sat outside on a wall. They said they were leaving. I made them sit down again, and I cried. I said I wanted to go back to school.

Marie-Rose and I went to a speech by the warden about rules and drugs and prejudice. I talked to some people in The Halls bar, but mainly I sat and felt sad. I can't stand the thought of the amount of time I've got to spend here.

Monday 3rd October 1988, University

Mrs. Deverson, the Italian tutor, has lovely eyes: deep dark brown.

Mr. Greaves, the German tutor, was worried that I didn't have A Level German. He rang Mr. Wolfe, the French tutor who admitted me to the university. I have to go and see Mr. Wolfe later.

At the Freshers' Fair, there was a Lesbian and Gay Society stall with a 'Lesbians are Out and Proud' banner.

Went to see Mr. Wolfe. He said I was a good linguist, with an excellent grade in Latin. He thought there'd be no problem with the German. Mr. Wolfe is very good looking, with a brill haircut, and brill clothes.

When I got back, the Christian Union had put leaflets under everyone's door. The girl in room 7 asked me if I was a Christian.

"... No." Bit sad, eh? First denial.

Set up my dartboard. Marie-Rose and I played a game. I won.

Several of us walked down to the Students' Union for the intro week beer tasting night.

Tuesday 4th October 1988, University

Joined the University Theatre group. They were pleased when I said I could design posters.

Bought £90 bus pass for the whole year.

Caught the bus to the Students' Union for the intro week cabaret night.

Wednesday 5th October 1988, University

Letter from Mrs. Deverson in my pigeonhole to tell me she's my personal tutor. Brilliant!

Bought Women's Minibus card (£5).

The Halls barn dance in the dining room. Did two dances. Shattered.

Thursday 6th October 1988, University

First ever lesson was French language with Mr. Martin.

Italian meeting with Mrs. Deverson. She is ever so attractive. ... Doesn't take me long, does it?

Got back 4pm. Marie-Rose has a mini dust pan and brush. She was dusting her mat with it. I laughed and laughed at her and told her I would write it in my diary.

7:30pm went with Anthony Hill to the modern languages department cheese and wine party. Mrs. Deverson came over to speak to me, like I'd hoped she would. I asked her what personal tutors do. All the time I was looking into her beautiful brown eyes, and going red.

At the end, about 10pm, as a few teachers were leaving, I asked Mr. Wolfe where the bus stop was. He suggested I come to one of the halls of residence bars with them, then someone might give me a lift back to The Halls.

Someone bought me half a beer—a French assistant called Ysabel. We haven't even met yet. Mr. Wolfe showed me around some of the lovely old wooden rooms by the bar. A group of us stood about talking till 10:50pm when Mr. Wolfe and another French teacher offered to walk me back.

On the way, I asked Mr. Wolfe if he remembered Miss Williams yet. The other teacher said he did. Mr. Wolfe said he had looked up her file after I'd mentioned her at the Open Day. I asked what she was like.

Mr. Wolfe: "Hard-working."

"What did she get in her degree?"

"A 2:1."

"Which hall did she live in?"

Mr. Wolfe thought she might have lived in a house. He said I should ask the French secretary for her file. ... Wow.

The other bloke got to his house. Mr. Wolfe and I were on our own. He said, "You're asking some pretty blunt, obsessive questions. Why?"

"I'm interested. ... She's lovely."

"Have you got a crush on her?"

"... If you like. ... That was a pretty blunt question as well."

"I didn't mean it in a cruel way."

He said he knew exactly how I felt. There were a couple of teachers at his school he wished he'd kept in touch with and could now say to them "Look what a good job you did."

Oh wow, a man with feelings.

We got to The Halls 11:45pm. I felt really happy.

Friday 7th October 1988, University

Asked the French secretary if I could see Miss Williams's file. She didn't think she had anything, and told me to come back on Monday.

Asked the Italian secretary if I could see Miss Williams's file. She told me to ask Mrs. Deverson.

Mrs. Deverson (those eyes!) produced a card with not much information on it. But I now know what town she comes from (wow). And I learnt that she started doing Combined Studies, then changed to Modern Language Studies, and that she graduated in 1977. That makes her thirty-three-ish. I wish she were younger. There was no photo. What a shame.

Phonetics class at 12:30pm. Very, very interesting.

8:45pm disco at the Students' Union.

Saturday 8th October 1988, University

Letter from Mum's dad.

Started knitting red jumper for Louise's baby.

Student Union for Julia Fordham in concert. She was absolutely brilliant. Two encores. Waiting for the Women's Minibus back, Julia Fordham was right by me. I asked her for her autograph. She asked me my name!

Sunday 9th October 1988, University

Wrote to grandparents (Mum's).

Monday 10th October 1988, University

Hardly understood a word in the German oral lesson. Never mind.

...

Rang Louise about Mum's parents wanting to meet us. She wasn't at all keen. Mum would be furious if she found out.

5pm driving lesson. I did terribly.

Tuesday 11th October 1988, University

Invitation to school Prize Day, 25th November.

This morning saw Mr. Wolfe coming upstairs. Felt really silly.

Paid this term's accommodation bill money (£420) to Miss Chappel, The Halls secretary. She's blind. That must be awful.

In the afternoon lecture I discovered that André Gide was obsessed with little boys.

First French conversation lesson. Absolutely brilliant. Love Ysabel. She is hilarious and so interesting.

Thursday 13th October 1988, University

In the French language lesson Mr. Martin gave me my first piece of work back. "An excellent translation." I was over the moon.

Disgusting homework for German.

Not including money put aside for driving lessons, I have 65p in my purse and £8.50 in the bank.

Sat in the Charleston Building till 5:30pm, working. The girl I saw sitting at the Lesbian and Gay Society stall came with three other girls to get something from the sweet machine. I see her now and then. She fascinates me. She has a skinhead haircut. It's brilliant.

Wrote to the School Old Girls' Guild to ask for details of events.

Friday 14th October 1988, University

3pm I went up to Mr. Wolfe's office to ask him if I could retake my French A Level. He put his head in his hands and said he'd never heard anything so ridiculous. He added, "You do get some strange ideas, don't you?"

I asked him about Miss Williams's file.

He said he wasn't prepared to let me see personal info like that. "I think you've gone too far with this obsession. Quite frankly I think it's unhealthy."

He said I couldn't be right in the mind and I should wash it out of my hair, concentrate on my future, on my degree, and on my social life.

When I left his office I really felt like I just didn't care about anything.

Monday 17th October 1988, University

Couldn't do anything smoothly. In the middle of the three-point turn a lorry couldn't get past me, so I reversed back sharply and banged the curb. I failed my driving test again.

Saw Mr. Wolfe going up on the paternoster. He didn't see me. I think he's lovely.

Felt very upset about my driving test. Decided to have all my hair cut off. It's *so* short now.

10pm went to The Halls bar. Bought half a pint of beer (35p). Got talking to Anthony Hill. We went out onto the grass. He showed me his back-flip and walking on his hands. He invited me back to his room for a tomato Cup-a-Soup. We listened to music and talked.

Wednesday 19th October 1988, University

I now have £1.74 in my purse and 50p in the bank to last me till the end of the month.

Thursday 20th October 1988, University

Went up in the paternoster with Mrs. Deverson. I didn't need to go up. I asked her when you have to inform the exam board that you're taking an A Level. She replied moodily, "How should *I* know?!"

"You're a teacher."

In an equally moody voice: "No I'm not. I'm a university lecturer" as if I'd insulted her.

She asked me what A Level I was wanting to do. When I said "French" she looked confused. I said I wanted to get an A. She replied, annoyed, that I was past that stage now, and just got off at floor eleven.

Arranged an overdraft of £20.

The German assistant from school, Marion, is now studying here. I was talking with her and Tonya after class. I asked Marion if she kept in contact with anyone from school.

She said, "Just Mrs. Clifton."

"What about Miss Williams?"

"No."

"Who was your favourite teacher?"

She didn't have one. Not many of the teachers spoke to the assistants.

Put up my large Miss Williams photo poster on the wall by my bed. Marie-Rose didn't say anything about it. This was the first time I'd seen a photo of Miss Williams since 25th July.

Friday 21st October 1988, University

Washed my rat's tail for the first time ever.

Put up on the wall by my bed twenty-five photos of school, my designs of the French teachers' names, three postcards of school from the school shop, and a medium-sized photo poster of Miss Williams.

When I got back later, I was told that Mum's parents had come at 6pm to visit me as a surprise.

Saturday 22nd October 1988, University

Met Louise at the station 11:20am. She's grown a little bit bigger. She thought the jumper I knitted for her baby was lovely. We went round town and saw *A Fish Called Wanda* at the cinema.

When Louise was in bed, and I thought she wasn't looking, and the light was out, I kissed my two fingers and pressed them against Miss Williams's lips.

Louise said, "Pervert."

Clocks back an hour at midnight.

Sunday 23rd October 1988, University

10:08am there was a knock on the door to say there was a man downstairs, waiting to see me. We thought they'd forgotten to change their watches, but they just wanted more time with us.

Grandpa was taller and younger than I had expected. He said I looked just like Dad. Grandma was so small and sweet. They gave us each a toy dog, a wooden pot, real silver charms, a real corral necklace, and a purse with £12 in it.

They took us out to lunch. We talked about Mum. They said they didn't know why she is like she is and why she is so angry with them. They said she used to be beautiful and extremely popular. They turned up at our house when we were seven and eight, and Mum told them she didn't want to know them because she had had an unhappy childhood. They didn't understand. Auntie Mary has never tackled Mum about this because she didn't want to get involved.

Monday 24th October 1988, University

Postcard from Janusz, the security chap at McDonald's. How sweet. Where did he get my uni address from?

Tuesday 25th October 1988, University

On my way to French conversation, Mr. Wolfe's door was open. Looked in because he's so handsome. He saw me.

Ysabel is such an attractive person, brilliant unique personality. She was talking about going to the Phoenix Theatre on Monday to see a French film, and we should meet her in the Phoenix bar at 8:30pm. Monday is Halloween. After the lesson, without Ysabel hearing, people were saying they were going to Halloween parties on Monday instead. So, I might have Ysabel all to myself.

Wednesday 26th October 1988, University

Saw Mrs. Deverson at the paternosters. Her eyes are out of this world.

Thursday 27th October 1988, University

Before going to the French Society cheese and wine evening, I drank two mugs of cider given to me by Gabrielle, who lives in the room next door to me. It began at 7:30pm. The French Soc president is very pretty. Had two glasses of wine. Spent most of the evening talking to Marion, last year's German assistant from school. Asked her loads of questions about Miss Williams. She said, "You're fascinated by her."

When it was dying down, about 9:50pm, Tonya, Marion, Jerry, some others from the course, and I went to one of the halls of residence bars. I had two pints of lager. I was getting pretty drunk. I put my arm round Marion and asked her more questions about Miss Williams. She told me that Miss Williams was a mystery, that nobody knew anything about her. She lived miles away, nobody knew if she had a boyfriend (ouch), if she was engaged, or divorced, what she did at the weekends. She never talked about herself.

All through the evening I kept asking Marion if she could remember anything else about Miss Williams. She kept shouting "Nooo!" She was amused, though. She said I will have to write to Miss Williams and ask her to send me her curriculum vitae.

I asked Marion, "Do you love Miss Williams?"

"No."

"Why?"

"I don't prefer girls."

I had my head on Marion's shoulder, and I asked her to ask Miss Williams if she liked me. I made her promise. Everyone started teasing me, saying "Miss Williams hates you." And I kept screeching "Nooo!" really loudly every time they said it.

Ysabel was in the bar. She was looking at me, then covering her eyes with her hand, to tease me, as if to say she didn't want me there.

The bloke who walked back with Mr. Wolfe and me on the 6th was there. He looked at me curiously from time to time.

11pm they decided to ring a taxi for me. It couldn't come till 11:30pm, so they laid me down on a table to wait.

Jerry and a friend of his took me back in the taxi.

Friday 28th October 1988, University

Felt OK when I woke up—if not a little silly. Had a personal tutor meeting with Mrs. Deverson from 12:05pm to 12:30pm. She was nice to me. I was so relieved. She said I really took her aback the other day when I mentioned retaking French. She asked why.

"Because I wanted to be a French teacher and I don't want to tell my pupils I got a B."

"You might end up teaching in a school where you're more concerned with getting the pupils to pay attention."

"I'm going to teach in my old school."

"What makes you so sure there'll be a vacancy?"

"I can wait."

"Or that they'll accept you?"

"That's why I have to get the best results I can."

She said I seemed very preoccupied with my past.

I replied sharply, thinking she'd been talking to Mr. Wolfe. "What makes you say that? … I love my past." I felt really sad and was nearly crying.

She said I should concentrate on getting a first class degree.

I said I was more interested in A Levels than a degree.

"What are you doing here, then?"

"I want to be a teacher."

Got to phonetics class after they'd all gone in. Tonya and Marion were sitting two rows in front of me. Marion turned round and saw me. Tonya said, "Oh Natasha, you made it then. Are you alright?"

After the class I apologised and said I felt a bit silly.

Tonya said, "Don't feel silly. It was quite amusing really."

We all went to the Charleston Building café for lunch. Marion had to leave. I asked Tonya what Marion had said in the morning?

She said: It was really strange that I had a poster of Miss Williams on my wall (Jerry had told them).

Tonya said that Marion was intrigued by it.

Saturday 29th October 1988, University

Went to the Halloween party in The Halls bar for an hour. Talked to Paul the sub-warden. He said I could use his car to practise driving.

Sunday 30th October 1988, University

Went to the laundry. First time I've ever used a washing machine (35p). Ironed for the first time.

Monday 31st October 1988, University

Bought *A Little Respect* by Erasure (£1.99).

Phoned college at home about A Levels. Learned you have to register before the end of September for November A Levels. Very annoyed with myself for not having organised it before.

Got to the Phoenix Theatre 8pm. Ysabel arrived 8:38pm. No-one else from the French group came because of Halloween parties.

I offered to buy her a drink. She said bitter. I got us both a pint. We sat for a bit and talked. I asked her who her favourite lecturer was. She wouldn't tell me because it was unprofessional. She asked me mine.

"Mr. Wolfe."

"Why?"

"I think he's lovely."

She laughed and said she'd tell him. I hope she does.

I told her I'm an artist. She said she wanted to see my designs. Told her I did the *Gift of Friendship* poster for the University Theatre group. She seemed impressed. I said I'd do one for her.

Another French assistant arrived, with her boyfriend and his brother. I didn't like this. I wanted Ysabel to myself. She didn't pay much attention to me after that.

The film wasn't interesting. No-one enjoyed it. Then the four of them went off somewhere and I had to walk back. That upset me.

Wednesday 2nd November 1988, University

7pm Natalia invited Gabrielle (my next door neighbour) and me to her room. Natalia is Russian with a Jewish mother and Muslim father who had to run away to get married. Natalia and Gabrielle are law students in Strasbourg. They're studying law here for a year. We chatted about English and French slang and Judaism.

Saturday 5th November 1988, University

Huge parcel for me from Kate: an advent calendar and three presents in a 'Merry Christmas' bag.

About 11pm Natalia and Gabrielle came to my room. We had cider and crisps and talked about spiritualism until about 12:30am. Nice, but I wanted to work.

Monday 7th November 1988, University

After German language, saw Marion by the pigeonholes. She invited me to her party tomorrow. I was really happy.

Tuesday 8th November 1988, University

Was going up to French conversation in the paternoster, and Mr. Wolfe was waiting for the next one. I looked down and I'm sure he's going bald on top. I still think he's immensely gorgeous though.

7:20pm Mum and Dad phoned. I hate it when they phone. Dad told me that my old infant and junior school Christmas Fair is on the 24th November. Perfect. They worked out from my delight that I was coming home for the weekend. I hate it when they know things.

Had a pint of cider before going out. Took cider and white wine with me. Got to Marion's 8:10pm. Everyone else (Tonya, Jerry, etc.) was already there. Marion gave us rice, chilli con carne, spaghetti, sauce. I was drinking glass after glass of the cider and white wine.

I needed the loo and wandered downstairs. Tried one of the doors. It turned out to be the back door. And I locked myself out. Went round to the front and rang the door bell to get back in. They thought this was pretty funny.

Really enjoyed the evening. We all left about 10:45pm. Tonya and Jerry walked me home. Jerry said, "This is getting to be a habit." They took me up. I pointed at my three photo posters of Miss Williams on the wall, and said drunkenly: "There she is."

Tonya said, "Is that Miss Williams? She's very pretty."

They left me. I went next door and talked to Gabrielle for twenty minutes. She gave me an apple and went to bed.

I still wanted to talk to someone. Saw that Lucy's door was open ... so I walked in. Turned on the light. She wasn't there. So, I picked up her guitar, sat on her bed, and played it. A few minutes later she came back. She wasn't very pleased. I felt rather embarrassed. She kept asking, "What's the matter? You don't look very well."

I went into our room and sat on my comfy chair. A little later, Lucy came in, with Alison. They kept asking me what the matter was. Alison sat on the edge of my bed, and Lucy on a chair, which she pulled up in front of me. Alison was asking question after question: "Why can't you tell us? ... You'll feel so much better. ... Will you be embarrassed if you tell us? ..."

I just answered with a series of shakes and nods.

Somehow Alison said, "Have you just found out that you're a lesbian?"

I always laugh when people say things like that.

They were saying that it's nothing to be ashamed of, that "this isn't the 1930s," that I should talk to people who've been through the same, that I should join a group. It was really quite amusing.

Lucy asked about "the lady on the wall."

I told them that I love her.

They asked me what sort of relationship I wanted with her, saying that there are many different types of love.

I just kept repeating, "I love her."

This conversation went on for about an hour. Lucy kept getting up and looking at the photos.

Marie-Rose came back at 1:14am. I was crying by this time. Alison and Lucy left.

Marie-Rose wanted to know what was wrong. She said, "If they insulted you, I'll kill them." That made me feel so good. The drink was really wearing off by this time. All I told Marie-Rose was that I really missed school.

Wednesday 9th November 1988, University

Bumped straight into Lucy this morning, of course. She asked me if I was alright. I said so, and I apologised for having been in her room. She asked me again, "Is there anything you want to tell us?"

I replied, to tell her that she couldn't steal information from me while I was sober, "The drink's worn off now, eh."

At the Frederick Building pigeonholes I saw the girl who was sitting at the Lesbian and Gay Society stall at the Freshers' Fair. I went over to my pigeonhole and took note of which section she was looking at. They are ordered by first letter of your surname.

Tonya had invited me to her block's pancake and wine party at her halls of residence for this evening. I went. Everyone was really friendly. Tonya told me not to drink too much this time as there was no-one to take me back. I felt really bad about that. She asked me if I had *meant* to get drunk on Tuesday. I managed to avoid the question.

Thursday 10th November 1988, University

Bought Cornish pasty (60p), smoky bacon crisps (16p. What a swizz. They're meant to be 15p), and a Mars Bar (21p). That's the most I've ever spent on a lunch.

Wrote a letter to put in Natalia's pigeonhole in the dining room because she gets very upset when she has no letters.

Friday 11th November 1988, University

In phonetics, Tonya didn't say a single word to me. And afterwards they all went off to the library together. I sometimes get the feeling that Tonya's pretty fed up with me.

After dinner at 6:50pm Natalia invited Gabrielle and me to her room. She was *so* pleased with the letter. She said, "Natasha, I love you." She showed us a ball dress she'd bought and we talked about the Second World War, till 9:17pm.

Saturday 12th November 1988, University

Phoned the driving school 11:45am. Answering machine. I've never spoken on one of those before.

Gabrielle went through my German oral workshop speech with me. She speaks German, French, and English fluently.

I miss Miss Williams.

Sunday 13th November 1988, University

Met Paul the sub-warden by his car at 11am. He drove us down to the university, then I took over. We drove around campus and practised three-point turns and reverses for ages.

When we got back to The Halls I didn't know what to do. Was he expecting me to kiss him? I offered him petrol money. He said to buy him a drink some time.

Put another letter in Natalia's pigeonhole.

Got a reply from Natalia.

New single by Sigue Sigue Sputnik. It's brilliant. Buying it!

Monday 14th November 1988, University

Bought twenty Embassy (£1.49). First packet of cigarettes in ages.

Bought *The Writers' & Artists' Yearbook 1989*. A ticket to a fortune. I keep thinking I'm going to make pots of money out of my art. Fortune = Miss Williams.

Wrote to Emily. Sent her a cheque for £6 to get me three tickets for the school play on three separate nights. At the end of the letter I asked her to "give my regards to Miss Williams?"

Replied to Natalia.

Tuesday 15th November 1988, University

Saw a notice in the Students' Union to give blood. Thought that if I could put myself through that, then I could put myself through getting a tattoo.

The nurse took a blade with a sharp point out of a packet and before I knew what she was doing, she'd plunged it into my thumb.

It really hurt. Then she stuck a little tube in the hole and sucked out some blood to test it. It was OK.

Lay on a bed. They had to do it on my right arm because they couldn't find a vein in my left one. They stuck the tube in, which really hurt. The blood coming out felt really uncomfortable, too. The girl on the next bed to me was being sick.

The doctor asked if I'd like them to take the tube out of my arm.

"Yes!"

They only got about half of it. Had to lie down and rest for twenty minutes. Was then given squash and biscuits.

After French conversation Ysabel asked me where her picture was. I said it would be ready for next week.

Wednesday 16th November 1988, University

11:30am driving lesson. We spent most of it parked, with him telling me what was wrong with my driving. Lessons have gone up 50p to £9.50.

Bought *Success* by Sigue Sigue Sputnik, and *So In Love With You* by Spear of Destiny. Love it.

Joined the town library. Ordered *The Well of Loneliness* by Radclyffe Hall, and *The Love of Good Women* by Isabel Miller. I feel really stupid ordering books like that. What are they thinking? Amusing, though.

Worked in The Halls bar for the first time. Really good fun. A bloke called Spud bought me a drink. I had a bitter lemon.

Thursday 17th November 1988, University

I was sitting at the tables in the Charleston Building at lunchtime, writing a poem to my love, when Ysabel saw me and came to talk to me for no reason. I like that.

Knocked on Lucy's door to ask for two five pence pieces for the laundry. We ended up talking for fifteen minutes. All the time I kept thinking of the other Tuesday. I think she feels uncomfortable talking to me. It's very amusing.

I think Ysabel is absolutely wonderful. Those eyes! I think it's her voice more than anything.

Friday 18th November 1988, University

Driving instructor spent most of the lesson talking again. I was nearly crying. He doesn't think I should pass because I would be dangerous.

Finished my design for Ysabel.

Saturday 19th November 1988, University

Phoned Louise. Janusz the security bloke from McDonald's had asked her for my address as a surprise.

Sunday 20th November 1988, University

At lunch Natalia bet me a KitKat that Sigue Sigue Sputnik wouldn't be higher than no.20 in the charts.

Spent most of the afternoon in bed listening to my Walkman, looking at my photo posters of Miss Williams (... and most of the morning).

After dinner Natalia came up to my room to listen to the charts. I owe her a KitKat.

Monday 21st November 1988, University

Listened to *Success* by Sigue Sigue Sputnik a few times to calm my nerves. Driving test 1:55pm. The examiner said to turn right. I didn't stop close to the white line in the middle of the road. Cars were overtaking me on the RIGHT.

"The reason they are overtaking you on the right is because you are incorrectly positioned."

Thanks.

This was closely followed by a FIVE-point turn.

Asked the driving instructor to drop me off in town. Decided I was definitely going to get a tattoo. I found a place on the top floor of the arcade.

The tattooist was really friendly. I wrote down what I wanted, and kept asking him how much it hurt. I can't believe how brave I was. He wrote on my left wrist in pink pen, and dipped the needle machine in black stuff. It wasn't too bad at first, then started to get painful. I closed my eyes and squeezed his knee tightly with my right hand.

Blood came up through the holes. It was sore, but bearable. It cost £5. He was intrigued about Miss Williams, but I didn't tell him anything. He put a tissue and Sellotape over it. I now have 'MISS WILLIAMS' tattooed on the top side of my left wrist.

Went into a typewriter shop and asked if they sold mini tape recorders. They did. Bought one for £24.95. It had a cassette with it. So exciting. What a bargain. I love it.

Fetched *The Well of Loneliness* from the town library.

At dinner I saw Marie-Rose, left my place, sat down by her, and looked her in the face, sadly.

"What? ... You failed your driving test? ..."

I nodded.

She put her arm round me. She's never done that before. Really nice.

Tuesday 22nd November 1988, University

Had just picked up and opened *The Well of Loneliness* to start reading it, when Marie-Rose came in. ...

At the end of French conversation class I gave Ysabel her design. She really liked it. I love her mannerisms. *Wow.*

After Italian language lab I realised I'd forgotten to give Ysabel my homework. Went back up to her room. She said, "I really like that, you know. It must have taken you ages."

At dinner there was a massive food fight—mainly boiled potatoes. It was hilarious. One of the dinner ladies was trying to stop it. She was furious. They gave brooms to some of the boys (second years) who were doing it and closed the doors to the kitchen, so that those who were waiting couldn't have dinner until the mess was cleared up.

Read *The Well of Loneliness* to page 38.

Wednesday 23rd November 1988, University

This morning I was coming out of my room and saw Alison running out of Lucy's room. She looked round guiltily—as if she'd been there all night—and caught my eye. Love it.

Went up to floor eleven to hand in some German. Was just getting into the paternoster when I realised that the girl who was already in there was the one from the Lesbian and Gay Society stall at the Freshers' Fair. As we went down I felt really self-conscious. She must have sensed it. She has gorgeous light brown eyes.

Thursday 24th November 1988, University > Home

After Italian I went up to floor twelve to see Mr. Wolfe. He invited me into his room.

"What can I do for you?"

"You know you said you were going to write to Miss Williams?"

"Did I?"

"Well, you said it sort of jokingly. Did you?"

"I can't even remember saying it. ... No, I didn't. ... Why? ... Was I meant to?" (astute. Love it)

"No, no, no. Of course not."

"How's term going?"

"Great."

"Been home yet?"

"I'm going home tonight. ... I'm going to school on Friday."

"Oh?"

"Speech Day."

He suddenly bent over to look at my wrist. I'd forgotten. I hadn't made it visible on purpose. I stuffed my hand in my coat pocket and muttered, "Shit," embarrassed. He definitely heard that. He said something about lots of people going round with tattoos. Brilliant.

Caught the 4:51pm train. Arrived about 6pm. As I was walking up the steps, I became aware that the person in front of me was Miss Byron. I followed her into the main station, went up to her, and said cheerily, "Hello, Miss Byron." She was going late night shopping in town, and I was going to the bus station, so we walked together. Nice.

She asked me how I was getting on.

I said, "Great. But I would much sooner be at school."

She thought that was lovely. I kept saying it. I think she thought I was joking.

Got to my old infant and junior school 6:50pm for their Christmas Fair. I joined the queue for the hot dogs. When Mrs. Robinson was making mine, I asked her, "Do you remember my name this year, then?"

She said, "Yes. ... Natasha."

I asked her if she remembered me when I was five.

She did.

"What was I like?"

"Stubborn."

When Mrs. Robinson saw me coming for a third hot dog, she laughed. I asked her about Mrs. Berk. She's a headmistress now. ... I said I had Mrs. Berk in the second year and I didn't like her.

"Why not?"

"Because I wanted to stay with you."

The other two teachers selling hot dogs patted Mrs. Robinson on the back, laughed, and said, "Aww."

I asked Mrs. Robinson, "What's my surname?"

"Holme, of course. And your sister's Louise. Does your dad still cycle to work?"

I said, "I'll see you next year."

Friday 25th November 1988, Home

Caught the bus 11:21am. Got to school and hung around till 12:15pm. Some of the teachers saw me and didn't look surprised. ...

I saw Miss Williams's back as she went to lessons after break. She was wearing her grey jacket. I noticed even from my spot on the window sill in the sixth form block how long her hair had grown. It looked absolutely lovely.

Went looking for my Miss Williams picture. It wasn't there. I was so annoyed. Went up to Miss Williams's form room—cautiously. I was so nervous. Lifted up the poster that she'd stuck over the holes left by my drawing pin message. You can make the message out.

Hung round the art rooms. Mrs. Gatwick went to fetch Mrs. Harrison for me. Mrs. Harrison wasn't pleased. She said she was busy. I asked her about my picture. She was not nice at all. She said it had been framed and put up, and taken down again at half term, and if I had missed it, it was my own fault. Charming.

She asked if I wanted it back. I did.

Caught the bus back to town 2:25pm. Bought a vase for Marie-Rose because her boyfriend keeps buying her flowers and she has to put them in a glass.

School Prize Day this evening. Bit nervous. Bit excited. Took my mini tape recorder, camera, spare film, Walkman.

Caught the 5:35pm bus. Went into the Bull and Sparrow next door to school at 6pm. Bought a double Scotch (£1.56), and half a lager (56p). Sat down at a far table. Listened to my Walkman. Drank the double Scotch down in one.

Went into school. Up to the balcony in the assembly hall. By this time I was feeling extremely dizzy. All the time I was thinking, "Can Miss Williams see me?" Sat in the third row back.

I taped a bit of Miss Byron's speech. It ended about 8:30pm. Miss Byron said that only white ticket holders could go to the buffet. I was stunned. I was heart-broken. Saw Cass and some others. They said they were going into the buffet anyway. I was extremely happy about that. Then Miss Halsie and the other Latin teachers invited us in.

The drink was really wearing off, so I excused myself and went back down to the Bull and Sparrow for half a lager. Still felt sober, so had another half. Felt reasonably tipsy. Went back to school.

Walked into the dining hall cautiously, looking about me. Didn't see her. Saw Mr. McKay and talked to him for ten minutes. Taped some of it.

Went round talking to the odd person, and to Mrs. Duffield. At one point I saw Miss Williams through some heads about a metre and a half away. I quickly turned my back and started talking to Lee and Philippa.

Miss Williams worked her way through the crowd very close to me, so I saw her profile. She didn't look my way. She was *so* close. She must *definitely* have seen me.

I walked round and round looking for her again. Couldn't see her. People were leaving about 9:30pm. So, I walked round by the staff room. I suddenly went up and rang the bell. Mr. Gilbert answered. Mrs. Gatwick was there as well.

I said, "Is Miss Williams in there?"

He said, "I don't think so."

"Are you *sure*?"

"Do you want me to look under the tables?"

Mrs. Gatwick said it was foggy, so she would have left as soon as possible to get home safely.

I walked to the main door and put my head on the post by the stairs and started crying *a lot*. Miss Byron came up to me and asked what the matter was.

After some hesitation I said, "... I just want to come back to school."

She laughed in a way that sounded pleased.

Two of the Lower Sixths walked past and asked if they could help. They offered to give me a lift home.

Got in and went straight upstairs.

I love her.

Saturday 26th November 1988, Home

Caught the bus to town about 3pm (67p). Went to the tattoo place by the shopping centre. A bloke was having one done, so I went to Boots.

At school yesterday I saw a notice for people to bring toiletries for Miss Williams's stall at the Christmas Fair.

In Boots I bought creme bath (99p), talc (75p), liquid soap (95p), four-pack of Palm Olive (78p), pink sponge (55p), green bath set: tumbler (75p), face cloth (69p), soap dish (75p), toothbrush holder (85p), soap container (75p). (Later, I put these in a cardboard box, and put in also a box of tissues from the cupboard under the stairs, and talcum powder that Sharon gave me for Christmas a few years ago.)

Went back to the tattoo place. Had to wait another half hour. The bloke still having one done asked me if I'd had one before. I showed him.

"Who's that?"

"My French teacher."

"I'm not trying to be funny, but does anyone ever take the piss out of your accent?" They thought it was hilarious that a public school girl had a tattoo.

While I was waiting, the tattooist asked what I wanted. I just said I wanted her name again. (Really I wanted 'I LOVE MISS WILLIAMS' across the back of my hand. I didn't say this because there were four people present.)

"Have you got a crush on her or something? ... She's not going to tell us."

It was my turn at 5:10pm. I sat in the chair and told him exactly what I wanted. He said he wouldn't do it on my hand because one day I'd regret it. I assured him I wouldn't. But he refused.

So, I asked him to add 'I LOVE' to the 'MISS WILLIAMS' on my left wrist.

He did it. It cost £2. The lettering is not the same. And the letters are too far apart. But never mind, it's too late now. It hurt more than I remembered. Lots of nice blood.

Mum gave me a bag of tuck (which was sweet of her): chocolate, nuts, crisps, etc.

Sunday 27th November 1988, Home > University

Lounged around on my bed listening to *Always On My Mind* by Pet Shop Boys, looking at my Miss Williams photos—my favourite occupation.

Started on Mrs. Duffield's Christmas card.

Got back to The Halls 9:45pm. I wish everything were as it used to be. I just want to go back to school.

Read *The Well of Loneliness* to page 79. I love this book.

Monday 28th November 1988, University

FOUR YEARS since I decided on my aim in life. And I still haven't changed my mind—naturally.

German tutor was away, so no German language lesson. Instead I lay down on the comfy chairs in the classroom, listening to my Walkman, and looked at my Miss Williams photos.

After Italian I went to the cashpoint and used my card for the first time. It was dead easy. I changed the number to the first four digits of Miss Williams's phone number. Love it.

Bought more toiletries for Saturday: bubble bath (69p), two pots of cotton buds (2 x 26p), and a bag of cotton wool (29p).

Gave Marie-Rose the vase. All she said was, "Oh, I need that."

Read *The Well of Loneliness* to page 158.

The scab has started falling off the 'MISS WILLIAMS' part of my tattoo.

Tuesday 29th November 1988, University

Saw Tonya 12:30pm. She invited me to come with them to the Phoenix Theatre tonight. I was *so* happy. She does like me.

Went into town, to a shop that sells everything for the home. Saw a pair of bathroom scales and thought how funny it would be if I bought them for Miss Williams's stall. So, I did (£5.99).

And a nail brush (25p), pack of two toothbrushes (29p), two green flannels (2 x 25p), pack of five razors (22p), and a make-up case (79p).

Phoenix Theatre with Tonya and Marion. They had half a cider each. I had a Coke.

Got back about 8:30pm and felt very happy. I love being with Marion and Tonya.

Read *The Well of Loneliness* to page 186.

Wednesday 30th November 1988, University

Went to see Mr. Greaves. Told him I'd read the first chapter of *Drachenblut* and didn't understand it, so couldn't do the essay. It was OK with him.

Went into town. Bought two spray-cans of fake snow.

When I got back there was a letter from Emily. I was *so* excited. Her letter was fantastic. She wrote:

"Miss Williams, Mr. McKay, and all my friends say 'Hello.'"

And she wrote that Miss Williams wanted to know what lectures I had because she might have had them. I screamed, I was so happy. I even shed a tear. But then the letter was dated 24th November and Miss Williams ignored me at Speech Day. I don't know what to think, but I'm very happy anyway.

Sprayed 'Merry Christmas Marie-Rose and Natasha' on the window in our room.

Read *The Well of Loneliness* in the bath to page 232.

I opened my eyes under water for the first time.

Thursday 1st December 1988, University > Home

10:30am waiting on floor eleven to go down in the paternoster, Mr. Wolfe was in the next one—alone. I got in, feeling uneasy. He asked me about Speech Day. I said it was OK, but I didn't talk to her though. I said I was going to the school Christmas Fair on Saturday, and the Old Girls' Guild event the following Saturday. But he didn't seem interested, and we went down a few floors in silence. It was awful.

Went to the bank. Withdrew £133.06. Love it. Now I can flash some money about at the Christmas Fair.

Bought a bag of eclairs for Kate (her favourite), and some Christmas decorations, which I put up in our room.

Waiting for the bus, I saw Mike Ticknell, one of the second years from The Halls. He asked, "Where's my rock, then?" He'd asked me to get him some last week when I said I was going home for the weekend. Mike is quite posh and unattractive and always wears an old-fashioned suit with a waistcoat. He's so sweet and weird. I'd marry him.

Caught 4:51pm train home. Went shopping. Bought loofah (£1.95), roll of cotton wool (79p), and balls of cotton wool (62p).

From 7:30pm I kept trying to ring Emily. Got through 9:38pm. Asked her about Miss Williams. Emily said that Miss Williams had said that when Emily next saw or wrote to me, she was to say 'Hello' from her and that she was glad I was getting on OK. That's amazing. Too much.

Friday 2nd December 1988, Home

Met Sara for lunch in the Vaults. When she went back to work at 1pm it occurred to me that I might see Miss Williams as it was lunchtime, so I went into school ... but just hid in the library.

Bought a bottle of Teacher's Scotch whisky (£7.99) and a can of lager (92p).

Met Paulo, Kate's boyfriend, for the first time, in the King's Head. He's sweet, and a bit funny-looking. Kate was coming home for good on the 3:20pm train, so we went to meet her. She got off the train, walked straight up to me, and hugged me tight.

Saturday 3rd December 1988, Home

Got up 8:30am. School Christmas Fair today.

Before leaving, I had two Scotches.

Dad dropped me off at school 10:15am. I put my bag, coat, scarf in the sixth form block. Took my big box of toiletries and made for the hall.

Learnt from one of the Lower Fourths that Miss Williams's stall was in room 8.

"Is she in there?"

"No."

I went in. Mrs. Duffield was looking after Miss Williams's stall until she arrived at 12pm. I was quite glad that I would be able to go round the fair for a bit without worrying about bumping into her. I left my box of toiletries under her stall.

Miss Williams had another stall next to it: 'Guess the teacher from the baby photo.' I recognised Miss Williams's baby photo easily. A beautiful black and white photo that looks just like her. I love her. Her eyes are exactly the same, but her hair looks blonde. I photographed her baby photo.

Walked round the fair. Drank more Scotch and some lager, and felt very dizzy. Won some face powder and puff on the tombola, so kept it for Miss Williams. Spent £7.50 on the tombola at 50p a go, and won a bottle of wine too.

At 1:15pm, after hovering about outside room 8, I plucked up enough courage to go in. She saw me. Her face said, "Oh no," like she was shy or scared. I went up to her. I had the mini tape recorder in my back pocket. I switched it on. She thanked me for the toiletries. I gave her three more.

We had a long chat about university. I taped the whole conversation. She asked me where I was living.

"The Halls."

She looked really surprised. She said she'd lived in The Halls for all three years. I couldn't believe it. Miss Williams in The Halls? Just amazing. She liked it. She asked me if The Halls Ball was happening this year.

Miss Williams lived in the old house at the bottom of the garden from the house I'm living in. Her sister, five years later, lived in one of the blocks.

Someone asked Miss Williams if she wanted to buy a can of drink. I learnt that she doesn't like fizzy drinks.

Someone else announced that there was a snake in room 7 next door. We went to see. Some girls from her Lower Fourth form came too, and one of them put her right arm through Miss Williams's left one. She didn't seem to like that. I wasn't so much jealous as proud that they love her. They said Miss Williams should have the snake round her neck. She didn't want it. It's so strange that things like that that really annoy me about other people, don't annoy me about Miss Williams.

One of her Lower Fourths asked me, "What have you been drinking?" (!) She must have smelt it. ...

"Can you tell?"

"Yes!"

Miss Williams may have heard. She went back to room 8.

2:10pm I went to the flower stall in the quad outside the assembly hall and bought a pot of mixed flowers (£3.95). I asked the bloke to take them to Miss Williams and say they're from Natasha. He found this really amusing. I fled and walked around the school.

I saw Miss Williams in the cookery room, having something to eat. I then saw her go back to her stall. So, I returned to the flower bloke and told him she was there.

He went off and gave her the flowers. I watched through the window, but could only see her back. I asked him what she said.

"She looked very surprised." The people around her were asking her what I wanted.

Walked around the fair some more. Talked to Mr. McKay and some of the other teachers.

Made a £5 bid for a plate Mrs. Gatwick had designed with the school crest on, which I won, because no-one bid higher.

The tombola stall had two items left: black tights and a bottle of wine. Miss Byron and I bought half the remaining tickets each. I won. I get the impression that Miss Byron isn't very fond of me after Speech Day.

3:45pm I was hanging about outside room 8, and eventually went in. The plant pot of mixed flowers was standing on the window sill by her stall.

She was wearing a black, pleated skirt, green sweatshirt with little coloured figures on, and a grey suede jacket—none of which I'd seen before. She was wearing make-up: pink-red lipstick and mascara. I so much prefer her without it. She doesn't look right with it on. Her natural features are more beautiful than anything she could add.

I just hung about by the stall as she and some of the girls in her form packed away. She didn't even look at me. At one point she was taking up the paper that she'd put down on the tables for her stall. I lifted up the end and had the Blu-Tack in my hand. She said, "Put that in the paper, Natasha, I'm throwing it away," still without looking at me.

I went and sat on the window sill outside room 8, as Miss Williams and some girls went to and from the staff room, carrying boxes.

When Miss Williams wasn't there, I asked the girls what happened about the flowers. They said that when Miss Williams came back, they told her that a bloke with flowers had come in twice for her. They said they had thought they were from a man. That made me feel a bit strange, and even jealous of my non-existent competitor.

"How did she react? Was she annoyed?"

"Of course not. She was pleased."

"What did she say?"

"Nothing. She just went a bit red."

Wow. ... I can make her go red. That is *so*, so sweet. At least she cares a little bit then. I love her more than ever. It's never going to go away. Nor do I want it to.

I kept sitting there waiting until she took the flowers, as then I would know she was leaving. So, I watched what she was carrying.

One time she came out and she smiled at me. I smiled back. Then suddenly I realised that the flowers had gone and so had she.

I went to the staff room and asked one of the teachers, "Is Miss Williams in there?"

She went back and checked. ... "No, she isn't."

When would I see her again?

4:50pm I went up to her form room (the needlework room). Not only were both the corridor door and her form room door unlocked, but they were both open as well. Maybe it was a trap? ...

I had my can of fake snow. Across the large window at the back of the room, I sprayed:

MISS WILLIAMS
I LOVE YOU

You couldn't see the 'I LOVE YOU' very well, so I sprayed it again, above.

I left school and walked around the outside. On the wall outside the cookery rooms, I sprayed:

I LOVE MISS WILLIAMS

And I sprayed the same again on the wall in the top playground. Cars and people were passing. I don't know if anyone saw.

I walked round the side of school. ... And I saw that somebody else had sprayed on the wall there a hand with the middle finger sticking up. ... So, they might think I did that as well. That would be awful.

Rang Dad to pick me up, but he was working in the garden and wouldn't. It was 5:17pm. There was a bus back at 6pm. So, I went to the bus station. It was pissing it down. I stood under a shelter. Decided to drink the rest of the Scotch, which I had in a little tonic water bottle. There were four or five measures left. I had put six in. I drank it down all at once.

Sat on a bench in the pouring rain with *So In Love With You* by Spear of Destiny blaring in my ears. I must have gone to sleep, because 5:50pm a girl from school came up to me. ...

"Are you drunk?"

"Why do you say that?"

"Because you're sitting in the rain."

The bus arrived. I got on. I sat down.

The next half hour was one of the best times of my life. It was bliss: pitch black outside, driving along, completely drunk, soaking wet, with my Walkman on really loud. I just sat there, with my head back, and cried and cried and cried. It was BEAUTIFUL.

The bus driver had to wake me up when we got there.

I headed for the petrol station, planning to get a fiver's worth of ten pence pieces to phone Miss Williams and tell her how much I love her. But Dad had come to meet me at the bus stop. That was sweet of him. I don't think he could tell that I was drunk.

I went straight upstairs when we got home and had two more Scotches.

Big mistake.

On my bedroom wall, I sprayed:

I LOVE MISS WILLIAMS

Appropriately enough, this was on the snow scene part of my mural.

Louise came in at one point and called me an "alchy."

I was lying on my bedroom floor, feeling ill. Then I was sick all over the carpet. Loads of it. Got a carrier bag and a ruler and scooped in as much as I could. Then got into bed and fell asleep with my clothes still on.

Sunday 4th December 1988, Home > University

Woke up at 2:30am. Didn't get back to sleep till 4:30am. I felt *so* ill. My stomach was killing me. Kept waking up. Tried to get out of bed about 9:30am to clean up my carpet and wall, but I couldn't. I was too dizzy.

Managed to get up 11am. Got the snow off my wall with a tissue, but it is still marked. You can still read it. Soaked a cloth and tried rubbing the sick stain for ages. It won't all come out. It's lighter than the rest of the carpet.

Listened to the charts and carried on designing Mrs. Duffield's Christmas card.

Dad drove me to the station. We sat in the waiting room. ... And up came the long-feared subject: "Are you going to the Christian Union this week?"

I dread that so much. It makes me feel awful. "No."

"Please. For me?"

"No."

"It upsets me, you know." He was pleading with me. He looked like he was going to cry.

I am ninety-nine percent positive he saw my tattoo. He was looking in that direction, so I looked away, pretending not to notice. I wanted him to see it.

Monday 5th December 1988, University

This morning I felt really bad about the snow. I kept looking at my watch to see what time she'd get to know about it.

In the German oral lesson, the assistant told me that the head of German wanted to see me. Suddenly I was so scared. I thought that Miss Williams had called her and that I was in deep trouble about the snow. ...

... But she went on about how I couldn't do Mr. Greaves's essay because I didn't have German A Level and couldn't understand, and that I never spoke in the oral lessons. ...

Sent off to Truprint for four more photo posters of Miss Williams.

All the scab is now off the 'MISS WILLIAMS' part of my
tattoo.

Read *The Well of Loneliness* to page 238.

Tuesday 6th December 1988, University

Went into town. Had two burgers. Looked for something to wear for
next Saturday.

Now that I've got my recording of Miss Williams's voice, I'm
more in love with her than ever.

Went back into town after lectures. Had another burger. I
can't stop eating.

Bought my first phone card (£2 for twenty units).

Wednesday 7th December 1988, University

After Italian, I went into town. Had a burger. Bought a gorgeous
jacket for next Saturday.

When I got back, I went to see Miss Chappel, The Halls
secretary, to ask her about Miss Williams. She remembered her
straightaway. It was wonderful. I was in there for about half an hour.
She answered every question I asked her. She even got out the
record box, which was all in Braille.

Miss Chappel had been the sub-warden, and one year had
had the room next to Miss Williams, so that Miss Williams had had
to put up with her music. Miss Chappel listened to The Carpenters,
Beethoven, Bach, and a piece of music called *Eye Level*.

She told me that Miss Williams was scared of birds, and had
a good sense of humour. Her friend was called Jane, who's now

married and about to have a baby. Miss Williams was a model student, extremely hard-working. She got a 2:1. She won an Arts prize for her hard work. She wasn't on The Halls committee because she preferred to concentrate on her work.

The best bit of info: There was a "young man who was after her affections," but she didn't like him, and thought he was a pest. He was very persistent. She just wasn't interested. Poor bloke. That's so sad. …

Miss Williams didn't do her year abroad, so she's only thirty-two. There's thirteen years difference in our ages, then.

Miss Chappel asked if I liked her (!!).

I said she was the loveliest person in the whole world, she was really kind, sweet, wonderful, perfect.

She said that Miss Williams was one of her very favourite students, and that she wasn't surprised that I like her so much.

Miss Williams doesn't write to her anymore, but they send each other Christmas cards.

She asked if I keep in contact with her.

I said, "No" and that I didn't think she liked me.

"Why?"

"I don't think she enjoys the amount of attention I give her."

She seemed to get my gist and told me that she was very fond of some of her teachers when she was at school.

I was close to tears.

She said that when I see Miss Williams again, I have to tell her to come and visit her.

I went down to see where Miss Williams lived for three years. It's a gorgeous house—really old and lovely. Knocked. There was someone called Hannah in Miss Williams's old room. I had a look round. She found it amusing, I think. It's so strange to think she lived there.

Thursday 8th December 1988, University

11am-11:22am went to see Miss Chappel again. I asked her about the bloke who was after Miss Williams. Miss Chappel had been thinking about what she'd said yesterday and she was a bit worried. She said she shouldn't have given me personal information, as I obviously wasn't as friendly with her as she'd first thought.

That *really* hurt.

"Did he give her presents?"

"I can't remember. ... Probably."

She said if you get presents from somebody you don't want to be friends with, it's even more embarrassing.

Did he love her? ... How long did he persist? ... What was wrong with him?

She couldn't remember.

I asked what her friend Jane was like.

"She was hard-working, serious." They weren't the type to go to discos, and only went to the bar occasionally. They went to the theatre and to concerts. They weren't dull, though. Jane used to go to the Anglican chaplaincy. She couldn't remember if Miss Williams went—maybe sometimes.

And she couldn't remember if Miss Williams had boyfriends.

Then she asked me if I had a boyfriend. (!)

I said no, I'd only been out with one bloke when I was fourteen and I didn't particularly want one.

She asked me, "Are you lonely, have you made friends?"

"Yes, I'm lonely. I have people to do things with, but nobody I'd miss."

"What about at school?"

I told her that I'd had a close friend, Jackie, in the first and second year, and that when Jackie broke friends with me I cried every night for two years. At this point I started crying, but she couldn't see.

Note from Louise to say that Mum and Dad are very angry about the mysterious stain on my carpet. I have better things to think about.

Natalia and Gabrielle and I went to The Halls Ball 8:50pm. Mike Ticknell called me "the beautiful Natasha Holme." Worked behind the bar with Ewan later. He was really drunk. He kissed me twice—quickly on the lips.

Caught fifteen minutes of Katrina and The Waves. They were brilliant. Danced with Ewan. Looked for Mike loads of times, but he must have left. Shame. Danced with Natalia.

Friday 9th December 1988, University > Home

Caught the train home. In Boots I had a look at the Christina Ortiz compact discs—beautiful. Bought *Stop* by Erasure.

Talked with Mum in the kitchen for a while. She didn't mention the stain on my bedroom carpet. When I went upstairs it had gone. ...

Caught 7:09pm bus. Went up to school to check the walls. The snow had been cleaned off. Phew. Maybe she doesn't even know? ...

Met Kate and Paulo in the Vaults 7:45pm. We were joined by a bloke called Bogey. I had a pint or two and got a bit dizzy. A girl two years below me at school told me she used to sit in assembly and stare at my finger nails.

Kate, Paulo, Bogey, and I went on to The Scotgate. Bogey bought me a pint of lager. I was crying. Kate took me outside. We sat on the wall and talked. I kept saying, "I want to go back to school."

Susannah joined us outside. I put my arm round her. I asked her if she liked my tattoo (All the scab has come off now). She didn't seem at all surprised by it (which is very bad manners, I think). I asked her to go to the staff room on Monday and say to Miss Williams, "Natasha loves you very much." She promised she would.

We left for the Vaults again about 10:40pm. Kate and Paulo walked ahead. Bogey and I stood in the High Street having the most passionate kiss. It was brilliant—delicious. I also got a love bite for the first time. We stayed there for ages. It was very hard to imagine it was Miss Williams because of his scratchy stubble.

Bogey and I eventually arrived at the Vaults 10:55pm and stood outside doing much of the same for five or ten minutes. It was great. I love Miss Williams.

We went in. I threw up all over one of the tables at the back.

They took me to the phone boxes in the High Street, but I couldn't manage. I just threw up again. So, Kate phoned Dad and told him I'd had too much to drink (Oh thanks, Kate) and that I was going to spend the night at their flat.

Saturday 10th December 1988, Home

On the phone last night Dad had made Kate promise to bring me home personally. We got there 12:50pm. Dad acted distant towards them. He had forgotten what he'd said.

Mum and Dad gave me a load of hassle: "How often do you do this kind of thing?" etc.

Louise saw my love bite, even though I'd tried to cover it up with concealer stick. She said, "Who gave you that ... Miss Williams?" I love it when she says things like that.

Got to school 3:55pm for the Old Girls Guild tea in the dining hall, by the conveyor belt. I was the only girl from our year. There were a few teachers, including: Miss Byron, Miss Tennyson, Miss Halsie, Mrs. Clifton.

I kept expecting Miss Byron or Miss Tennyson to say something about the snow. I asked Mrs. Clifton if Miss Williams was coming. She didn't think so.

I bought five strips of raffle tickets (£5) and won a box of mint chocolates. Miss Byron gave it to me. I was really pleased.

At the end I thanked Miss Byron for her A Level congratulations card. She did her 'Lovely to see you' routine.

6pm went to The Bull and Sparrow. Had a pint of Coke. Sat at the back, listening to my Walkman.

Towards 8:15pm I made my way to the boarding house, because Miss Williams had told me last week that she was going to their Christmas party, which was to begin at 7pm.

I sat down in the bike shed at the top of the garden, watching the door at the bottom of the path. It was really cold. I listened to my Walkman and got quite nervous.

At 9pm some teachers started leaving.

About 9:15pm Miss Williams came up the path with two other people. I couldn't see in the dark who the other two were. The two were turning left. Miss Williams was turning right. They all said good night to each other. She sounded happy.

I stood up, walked towards her, and said, "Miss Williams?" I couldn't see her face, just her outline, but she had on her gorgeous beige raincoat.

She turned round and she said, "Natasha," in a voice I later realised was in a semi-desperate, 'leave me alone' tone. But it sounded quite normal at first.

She just walked very fast, right back again, down the path to the boarding house.

I started to follow her, thinking she wanted to talk to me alone, down in the garden. But she just headed straight for the house and went in.

I was amazed. ...

I stood in the garden thinking, "She's got to come out some time."

Five minutes later it occurred to me that she'd have gone out another way. That upset me. I went down and stood outside the boarding house, leaning against the wall, and waited until 9:45pm.

I really couldn't believe what had happened. She just couldn't handle it. I hadn't had any alcohol all day. I thought she deserved a sober apology. I just wanted to say I was sorry.

Never before has she acknowledged my feelings for her in any way. Looking back, she seemed almost demented. I really wasn't expecting that at all. Does it mean she cares a little bit?

Sunday 11th December 1988, Home > University

Woke up with a sore throat, which later got very painful. Contemplated ringing Mr. McKay to tell Miss Williams I was sorry, but thought better of it. Finished Mr. McKay's Christmas card. And designed Mrs. Addison's.

Caught 8:27pm train back to uni. My throat was killing me.

Monday 12th December 1988, University

Very hard night. My throat was so painful, I kept waking up. My head felt like lead. I was upset because as yet I hadn't missed a single lecture, tutorial, class, anything.

Read *The Well of Loneliness* to page 254.

Tuesday 13th December 1988, University

Christmas card from Spud.

I made my first ever cup of tea.

Read *The Well of Loneliness* to page 282.

Wednesday 14th December 1988, University

Joint German and Italian Society ten pin bowling trip. On the coach I sat on the back seat with a second year called Ian Ashcroft. We had a good conversation all the way. He is twenty-seven.

We went to the pub before bowling and played pool. Ian got pretty drunk. On the coach back, he was trying to kiss me. Everyone else was sitting at the front. He saw my tattoo because I wanted him to, and asked who Miss Williams was. He said I could pretend that he was Miss Williams and that he would teach me some French. ...

Read *The Well of Loneliness* to page 323.

Friday 16th December 1988, University > Home

Mum and Dad came to pick me up 4:25pm. I watched to see their reactions at my Miss Williams photo posters. They didn't show any.

Met Kate and Paulo in the Vaults 7:45pm. I had a soda and black (30p). Bogey came in. Bit embarrassing. After a while he came by me, ruffled my hair, and said, "Alright, mate?"

I had a tomato juice and put *It's Over* by Level 42 on the jukebox (20p) and felt sad.

Karen came in. I sat down to talk to her. She said, "Let's see your tattoo."

"Who told you I had a tattoo?"

"I overheard someone say."

"What's it of, then?" I asked.

"It's a message."

"What's it say?"

"I don't know."

I showed her.

There was a drunken look of disbelief, after which she laughed and laughed. "And do you?"

"Yes."

She just kept laughing in disbelief. "Did it hurt?"

"Yes, it was very painful."

"Is it amiable or passionate?"

I didn't answer. She kept repeating that question and laughing. "Have you had any boyfriends? Are you of that tendency, or is it just her?"

I didn't answer.

Saturday 17th December 1988, Home

Rang The Boat House. They've no jobs left. Rang McDonald's. I was told to go in one day and ask. Dossed around listening to records and asking Miss Williams's photo to marry me.

Rang Susannah to see if she'd done what I asked her to do last Friday. She hadn't, of course. But I just wanted to know.

Sunday 18th December 1988, Home

Bought baubles, gift bows, box of After Eight mints, Ferrero Rocher, Napolitains, bunches of plastic holly and mistletoe. With all this, I made a Christmas card for Miss Williams. Much more fun than drawing. Took a few hours. Used wood glue.

Wrote a Christmas card to Karen as I'd promised her one on Friday.

Monday 19th December 1988, Home

Was in the post office for five minutes, sorting out presents and my card to Miss Williams, before joining the queue. My eyes fell on a lady at the front. ... I realised it was Miss Williams. ... And I just kept staring. ... Had she seen me? ... She was wearing a green jacket, grey trousers, and white wedges.

Read *The Love of Good Women* to page 80.

Wednesday 21st December 1988, Home

McDonald's shift 10am. Had to go on lobby. Yawn. The girl I was working with saw my tattoo and thought it was hilarious. I love my tattoo. Best thing I've done for years.

Thursday 22nd December 1988, Home

For the first hour or two at McDonald's I was dressing the burgers. Polly saw my tattoo. She kept saying, "I'm amazed." She went round telling *everyone*. It was very amusing. I like it when people talk about me. Darren Grace was the worst. He was making jokes like "Spank me, Miss Williams." Very funny, eh.

Friday 23rd December 1988, Home

Christmas card from Karen.

Saw something on TV that claimed that obsession falls between love and insanity. That's genius.

Saturday 24th December 1988, Home

McDonald's Christmas Party. I spent most of the evening talking to Patrick Jacobs. He told me that he can't bear to look at himself in the mirror. Patrick has hair like straw and his face is covered in spots.

When I got home, Mum and Dad and Louise and I sat in the living room for ages and talked and laughed. It was really nice. After about an hour, Mum said, "Where did you get your tattoo done?"

I'd felt sure they'd seen it.

Louise: "What tattoo?"

Mum: "The one on her wrist."

Louise didn't say anything else. Perhaps she just thought it was a joke. I just didn't reply.

Sunday 25th December 1988, Home

I was so tired. Nigel arrived at 10am. We had a traditional Christmas listening to *Now That's What I Call Christmas* LP and watching telly all day. It was great.

Monday 26th December 1988, Home

McDonald's shift 10am. I was on till for the first time. Loved it. Richard asked me if I had a boyfriend.

"Why do you want to know?"

A boy had asked him to find out because he wanted to ask me out. I like that. It's nice to feel wanted. He wouldn't tell me who it was, but it was someone shy.

Tuesday 27th December 1988, Home

I asked Richard about whoever it was who was wanting to ask me out.

"Has he been here today?"

"Yes."

"On the front or in the kitchen?"

"Kitchen."

"Is it Patrick Jacobs?"

"Yes."

Apparently Patrick asked Richard, and then Daniel, to ask me out for him. They both said no, and that he had to ask me himself.

Wednesday 28th December 1988, Home

Last night I had a terrible dream. It was one of those that you really believe is true. From a third of the way up my arm, to my hand, I had seven or eight tattoos—sentences that meant nothing, in black ink, that would be there forever.

McDonald's shift 10am. Richard told me that Patrick Jacobs kept asking him, "Is she still here? Has she gone yet?" It makes me feel so nice that someone thinks something of me. When I got back off my break, I heard Patrick in the back room asking Paul the same thing.

Friday 30th December 1988, Home

McDonald's shift 6pm. Dave Jarvis, one of the managers, kept asking me, "Are you a lesbian?" I gave no answer. He called me "Lez" all evening.

Janusz the security bloke asked me if I wanted to go for a drink with him some time next week. I was very happy at that. I said yes. I felt really wanted. It's a nice feeling.

There were a few of us in the back room. Dave Jarvis was washing his hands with liquid soap. He said to me, "Looks like spunk, doesn't it? ... Oh, you wouldn't know about that, would you?"

Got in at 3:05am. They weren't waiting up for me. Just a note to tell me to be quiet, and a torch.

Sunday 1st January 1989, Home

Out of interest I tried to cover up my tattoo with concealer stick and face powder. It didn't work at all. It looked like a black-green mess. I wouldn't have been able to cover it up on the back of my hand, then.

Read *The Love of Good Women* to the end. Page 31:

"I think women making love together is just a damn aphrodisiac idea."

Tuesday 3rd January 1989, Home

McDonald's shift 4:30pm. Polly didn't stop going on about my tattoo.

"Have you got a photo of her?"

"Yes, I've got some upstairs."

They had me go and get them. They said things like: "I can see why you're in love with her" ... "She's pretty" ... "She looks quite nice" ... "She has a very nice smile."

Dave Jarvis said, "Yeah, I see what you mean. I'd give her one as well." (!) That didn't make me feel angry. Even though he's a crude git, I felt proud. The "as well" made me feel a bit bad, though.

Janusz checked with me that it was OK for Friday. He seemed enthusiastic. I'm really looking forward to it. I really am. He's such a nice bloke.

Thursday 5th January 1989, Home
Bought Viz magazine for the first time (90p).

Friday 6th January 1989, Home
McDonald's shift 11am. On my break, as usual, I got loads of hassle from Polly and others about my tattoo. "Are you in love with her?" ... "Do you want to have an affair with her?" ... etc. I love it when they talk about it. I just don't answer.

Wrote to Mr. McKay, asking him to send me a school calendar for the spring term.

I put on my white dress and black jacket. Janusz picked me up 8:30pm. We went to his favourite pub, a quiet one.

He told me terrible things about the store manager having an affair, harassing the girls, and fiddling the wages. He bought me half a cider and a tomato juice. He had a pint of shandy and an orange juice and lemonade.

On the drive back, and sitting in his car outside my house, he was talking about the girl who broke his heart. I was getting worried about saying good night to him. So I asked him lots of questions about her, thinking that then he wouldn't want to kiss me.

I thanked him for a lovely evening and kissed him on the cheek.

He laughed.

Got in 12:11am. One misgiving about this evening: We spent the entire time talking about him, and not at all about me.

Sunday 8th January 1989, Home > University

Mum and Dad drove me back to The Halls 2:30pm. I unpacked and felt very lonely. Lay on my bed with my Miss Williams photos in the semi-darkness. I just want to go back to school.

There was a formal dinner at 6:30pm. I got there at 6:33pm. Everyone had already gone in. I felt so unwelcome. I just left. I went back and got into bed. I feel so unloved. I just want someone to love me, someone to care, a friend.

7:45pm Natalia and Gabrielle came to see me. Gabrielle gave me some Belgian chocolates, and Natalia gave me a little Russian doll.

Monday 9th January 1989, University

On my way to the Frederick Building, I bumped into Ian Ashcroft from bowling last term. He asked me out for a drink. I said I'd think about it.

Bought *Buffalo Stance* by Neneh Cherry.

Thursday 12th January 1989, University

1:45pm went to a meeting about *Le Bourgeois gentilhomme* theatre production because I knew Ian Ashcroft would be there. He asked if I'd thought about his asking me out for a drink.

"Yes. And yes."

He seemed very pleased and surprised—which I like.

8:30pm-10:30pm worked in The Halls bar. Spud bought me a drink again. I had tomato juice.

Friday 13th January 1989, University

A few days ago I had an excellent idea for Miss Williams's birthday present—a specially made real gold bracelet with an engraving. Today I thought I would have 'Miss Williams' written in little diamonds. I was thinking about £300. I hope I could afford it.

At dinner, Natalia asked me if I wanted to go to the cinema this evening. We decided on *A Fish Called Wanda*. But when we got there at 8:45pm, it had sold out. So, we went to McDonald's. Then to Kentucky.

We walked around town for ages, just talking. Natalia thinks that liking someone is simply that "there are more things you like about them than you dislike."

Other Natalia quotes: "I like being stupid in an intelligent way." ... "The only things that are stupid are things without a reason."

We got back 10:40pm. It felt like we'd been on a date. ... It didn't feel right that we just went back to our rooms.

Saturday 14th January 1989, University

Bought Barbara Streisand postcards for Natalia, who loves her.

Sunday 15th January 1989, University

7pm went to Natalia's room. Gabrielle and a couple of others were there. We had Russian champagne and something like caviar, which was gorgeous. Natalia said she was touched when I gave her the Barbara Streisand postcards.

Monday 16th January 1989, University

Went to Miss Chappel's office to pay my residence fees. I was pretty nervous. She asked if I'd had a nice Christmas. I had decided not to mention Miss Williams if she didn't. She didn't.

Tuesday 17th January 1989, University

Looked in my Frederick Building pigeonhole to see if Ian Ashcroft had written me a note yet. He had—inviting me round to his place tomorrow at 7pm. I replied, accepting.

No French conversation. Note on Ysabel's door that she's had an accident. ...

Wednesday 18th January 1989, University

Went to the print shop in town, asked about printing photos onto material. Was told it would have to be onto 100% polyester, and only in black and white.

Found a jeweller recommended to me by a jewellery shop. I described to him and discussed the bracelet I wanted for Miss Williams's birthday present. Decided on eighteen carat gold. I love it. He said it would cost about £400/£450.

And I ordered a silver ring (£25) and a silver bracelet (£75) for myself.

Went to the library to photocopy my diary in case I lose it. Wondered how photocopies of my Miss Williams photos would come out. They were brilliant.

Got to Ian Ashcroft's 7pm. There was a table in the middle of his room, where we ate. He'd set it up sweetly. We had red wine, Waldorf salad, risotto, banana custard (I left the bananas), cheese and biscuits. We were listening to Simply Red, The Communards, Simon and Garfunkel—all brilliant. He taught me how to play backgammon. It's good fun. Then Travel Scrabble. He was winning, but we had to go for the 11:15pm Women's Minibus. We missed it, so hung around outside the Students' Union, talking. It was really cold. He kissed me and we hugged. It was very nice—and warm. I love hugging.

Thursday 19th January 1989, University

11:30am Lucy told me that someone had phoned to say my sister had gone into labour. I was so excited.

French language test back: "87%—most impressive. Well done." Thrilled. The people on either side of me got 63% and 69%. Even 'Boffin' (the brightest student in our year) only got 84%.

Used a phone card for the first time ever. Mum had taken Louise to the maternity hospital 9am.

Friday 20th January 1989, University > Home

7:55am Mum rang. "You're an auntie." Louise had the baby last
night, about 9pm. … It's a girl. I was jumping up and down.

Bought some baby clothes and wooden baby blocks.

Got to the maternity unit 6:25pm. I was so excited. Nigel and
his sister were there. They left.

Louise was holding the baby, which she has now decided to
name Sophie. She was so small, and had her eyes closed the whole
time. She had dark hair, short at the front, and clumpy at the back.
Her hands and feet looked cold and wrinkled. She is gorgeous.
Louise said I could hold her. She wasn't possessive at all.

6:40pm Mum arrived. She loves the baby. Louise was in a
very happy mood with all her visitors and baby presents.

Two friends of Louise's arrived, so Mum and I went home.

Nigel and his sister came round to fetch Louise's stuff.
Louise rang home to speak to Nigel. Dad answered the phone. He
hadn't seen or spoken to Louise since she went into hospital, and he
didn't say a word to her on the phone now. Mum was furious with
him and shouted at him when they were upstairs.

Saturday 21st January 1989, Home

We rushed to the maternity unit for the beginning of visiting time at
3pm. Louise was hungry as she doesn't like hospital food, so Dad
went out and got her Kentucky Fried Chicken. Dad then paid a lot of
attention to Sophie—rather self-consciously. I got the impression he
was too scared of Mum not to.

Monday 23rd January 1989, University

Saw Ian Ashcroft in the Frederick Building. He invited me to the Phoenix Theatre on Wednesday.

Finished my 'get well soon' card for Ysabel, and birthday card for Mr. McKay.

A Rabbi came to visit Natalia in her room at her request. I stayed, out of interest. Discovered that Jews are supposed to discourage people from converting to Judaism because Jews have six hundred and thirteen laws to obey, whereas the rest of humanity has just seven.

Wednesday 25th January 1989, University

Photocopied my A4 photo of Miss Williams twenty-five times at the town library.

Was due at Ian Ashcroft's 7:30pm. The bus was so full, it drove right past. I was twenty minutes late. When I got there he was asleep. We walked to the Phoenix Theatre. The place was packed and the tickets had sold out. We went to the Odeon instead. Saw *High Spirits*. He made me buy my own ticket (£1.65).

We waited at the bus stop. The inevitable kiss which, in fact, I hadn't wanted to 'evit.' Not as good as last time, but still nice.

On the way back he kept asking me to his place for coffee and to stay the night. I refused. It was no temptation. I don't want to see him now, and that's a good excuse. You'd think if you had that in mind, you would at least pay for someone's cinema ticket, wouldn't you?

Thursday 26th January 1989, University

Between 3:15pm and 4:15pm stuck photocopies of Miss Williams's photo on floors three to eighteen of the Frederick Building, opposite the paternoster. It was really funny. My aim is to get people so interested in this photo that it appears in the Students' Union newspaper.

Friday 27th January 1989, University

After the French lecture 4:15pm, I went up on the paternoster, checking the photocopies of Miss Williams. They had only been removed from floors five, seventeen, and eighteen. On floor eleven it was in the bin, so I stuck it back up. On my way up, I saw the girl from the Lesbian and Gay Society. I heard her speak to someone. She sounded really nice and cheery. An interesting voice. She was on floor fourteen. I'll have to go and see what subject that is.

Saturday 28th January 1989, University

Worked in The Halls bar with Spud for the Bad Taste Party. I wore green shirt, orange cardigan, purple leggings, red socks.

Monday 30th January 1989, University

The paternoster was out of use today. So, before Italian I went up on foot to check the Miss Williams photocopies. All there except seventeen and eighteen again.

After Italian I was standing waiting at the lift with our Italian language tutor. He looked at the Miss Williams photocopy and said to me, "Do you know what the point to these pictures is? They seem to be on every floor."

I hesitated. My heart was beating really fast. I replied, "... It's a very nice picture though, isn't it?"

In town I made one hundred more photocopies of Miss Williams (£7.54).

Bought *Love Train* by Holly Johnson, *The Unforgettable Fire* LP by U2 because I want to record *Bad* on my 'Miss Williams' tape.

Tuesday 31st January 1989, University

Ysabel's back, with leg in plaster, and crutches. She said, "Thanks for the card, you. That was very nice."

Paternoster working again today.

Wednesday 1st February 1989, University

I usually see Ian Ashcroft before or after Italian. Managed to avoid him.

Bought large pack of dry roast peanuts for Gabrielle because she likes them.

Natalia told me she saw one of the Miss Williams photocopies when she was on the paternoster in the Frederick Building. She was so shocked. She said, "I wish somebody loved me that much." ... Later Natalia informed me that she was being sarcastic.

Thursday 2nd February 1989, University

This afternoon, going down in the paternoster, I saw someone had defaced the Miss Williams photocopy on floor three. Went back to look. She was wearing glasses, moustache, and a blacked-out tooth. It looked so funny, I had to laugh.

Friday 3rd February 1989, University

Went to the jeweller's to collect my silver bracelet and ring with 'MISS WILLIAMS' engraved on them. I was really excited. Loved them straightaway.

Sunday 5th February 1989, University

At dinnertime I noticed what beautiful eyes Hannah from Miss Williams's old room has. They took my breath away. Hannah was sitting with the members of the Christian Union. Interesting.

Monday 6th February 1989, University

I'm pretty sure our Italian language tutor thinks I'm the one who put the Miss Williams photocopies up.

Saw Ian Ashcroft for the first time since 25th January. I was going up in the paternoster, so I just said "Hello" and looked away.

Natalia is the first one to notice my silver bracelet. She absolutely couldn't believe it cost £75. Then neither could Gabrielle.

Tuesday 7th February 1989, University

At lunchtime in the Charleston Building foyer the Christian Union sang and gave talks. It was really good—especially looking at Hannah.

5:15pm went all the way up on the paternoster. Every single Miss Williams photocopy had been taken down. Poo. I stuck some more up on floors three to twelve, one in the toilets, and put one, folded in half, in every pigeonhole.

Wednesday 8th February 1989, University

This afternoon Marie-Rose announced that she was moving out to live with her friends. I shall love the privacy, but it just won't be the same.

Thursday 9th February 1989, University > Home

Bought a wooden teddy jigsaw for Sophie. Got home 5:35pm as a surprise. Mum was ever so pleased to see me.

6:45pm I phoned Michelle. About ten minutes into the conversation she asked, "What's all this about a tattoo?"

I was speechless. I couldn't think who'd told her. ... It was Kate. Brilliant that Kate's telling people. And Michelle is a blabbermouth.

Friday 10th February 1989, Home

Went round to see Louise 11:25am. She and Nigel had a massive argument.

Saturday 11th February 1989, Home

Bought two metres of white 100% polyester (£5.90).

Went to the tattoo studio. Got the same tattooist. Asked him to go over the 'MISS WILLIAMS' again as it was thinner than the 'I LOVE.' It didn't hurt too much this time. Cost £5.

Sunday 12th February 1989, Home > University

Rang Sara. She too asked me about my tattoo. She couldn't believe it, thought it was hilarious. Kate had told her. Sara said, "You're even madder than you were at school." I asked her about making a shirt for me. She said she would.

Michelle came for Sunday lunch. Louise and Sophie too. Michelle said that she hadn't really been listening ... but she thinks she might have overheard two of the younger girls from school saying that Miss Williams is engaged. My heart fell. It was like being thumped in the face. Such a feeling of despair.

3:10pm phoned Emily to try and find out if it were true. Discovered she's had a roller-skating accident and injured her pelvis, so hasn't been to school since the Christmas holidays. She sounded really excited when I asked her, but she didn't know. She'd ask someone at school, then write to me.

Louise saw my tattoo for the first time. She'd spotted it at lunch and thought it looked too neat to be just writing. She couldn't believe it. She said, "I don't know what to say."

I got back to uni 6:27pm. Walked to the Phoenix Theatre to see the second half of *Two In Twenty* (because one in ten sounds lonely)—a lesbian film. I sat at the back feeling really self-conscious.

Worrying: This was the first time I've seen women kissing and not felt odd about it.

Tuesday 14th February 1989, University

Letter from Grandma (Dad's mum): "I was puzzled about the baby you hurried home to see. Whose baby was it?" ... Great big fat whoops.

No Valentine cards. I don't feel very wanted.

This morning I used Luigi, the Italian department computer, for the first time. I typed my name in as 'Miss Williams.'

Wednesday 15th February 1989, University

I got a Valentine! I'm very happy. From the post mark I think it must be from Janusz.

Thursday 16th February 1989, University

Miss Williams crisis this evening. Had slightly bitter thoughts about how uncaring she is about what I'm going through, especially not having me as her form prefect last year. She really isn't very nice.

I have to remember that my love for her is *unconditional*. Whatever she says or does I'm to love her anyway. I'm slipping. The fire needs stoking up. I can't live without loving her, because I haven't got anything else.

Friday 17th February 1989, University

A bloke I talk to in the Wimpy saw my tattoo and asked me if I was gay. He said he was. Someone else did exactly the same yesterday. Two gay blokes who admit it. And both of them said they thought I was gay anyway because of the way I act and my mannerisms (? ...). The Wimpy bloke is twenty. His boyfriend is forty-five! I asked him if it was different kissing a boy to kissing a girl. He said it was the same except for the stubble.

Saturday 18th February 1989, University

Got up for breakfast to see if there was a letter from Kate. A few weeks ago I invited her to come and visit me today. She never replied.

10:50pm Gabrielle and I went to the sixties disco in The Halls bar. I was looking for Mike Ticknell. Gabrielle took me over to him. We all talked and danced until the disco finished at midnight.

Mike asked me back to his room for a hot chocolate (as I'd refused coffee and tea). He showed me last year's group photo of The Halls.

"How long have they been doing those?"

"Ages, I think."

Miss Chappel had told me she didn't have a photo of Miss Williams. I asked Mike to ask her if he could borrow 1976's and 1980's (Miss Williams's sister). I told him not to mention they were for me. He said he'd have a go.

We talked till about 1am. He walked me back. He asked me if I'd like to go out for a drink. I said I would. He'd meet me 8pm

Thursday in the foyer. I was really happy. Gabrielle congratulated me and shook my hand.

Wrote to Emily and asked if she could get me a ticket for the school play on Saturday 4th March. If Miss Byron is there I'm going to tell her what I did after the Christmas Fair.

Sunday 19th February 1989, University

Wrote to Grandma. Omitted to mention any baby.

Thought today I should get personalised writing paper, with Miss Williams photos round the edge. Thought also I'd get a bit of body piercing: nipples, vagina.

Monday 20th February 1989, University

Muslim stall in the Students' Union. I bought *The Quran: Basic Teachings* and *Islam and Christianity*.

Hustings for Vice President of The Halls. Candidates: Roberta, Fabio, an individual pork pie, and Terry's testicles.

9:30pm went down to ask Hannah (wow) if she was leaving Miss Williams's old room next year, because I want it. She wasn't in.

Tuesday 21st February 1989, University

We all have personal tutor appointments this week. Mine was at 11:40am today, with Mrs. Deverson. She asked me about my theatre poster designs, and about how I'm coping with literature essays if I can't read the German. Then she said there was a particular matter she wanted to talk to me about: "The photos."

I didn't catch on first of all.

"The photos that were up on various floors of the Frederick Building."

Oh, shit.

She said that some members of the language departments had recognised her, and were disturbed, worried, concerned to say the least. She said it was my personal life and shouldn't be put up on public display. She said it was my "affair." I laughed. And she hurriedly searched for another word.

"Would you like to explain?"

"I wanted to decorate the place. ... You'd understand if you met her."

"Well, I haven't met her."

"I think she's lovely." (I should have said "I love her.")

She said I should try to get more involved with the present and future.

In the dining hall I plucked up enough courage to go over and talk to Hannah. It's very hard to act naturally with someone you fancy rotten. The colour of her eyes is so beautiful. Light bright brown—wicked. I asked her where she was going to live next year. She said she's moving out.

"Why, do you want my room?" She said it like she knew I did.

"Yes. Are you definitely moving out?"

"Yes."

Those eyes!

Wednesday 22nd February 1989, University

2:30pm went to see *Le Bourgeois gentilhomme* at the Frederick Building Theatre. Their French is amazing. Ian Ashcroft is Monsieur Jordan, the lead part. Impressive.

Thursday 23rd February 1989, University

In town did quite a bit of various photocopying of my Miss Williams photos.

Roberta won Vice President of The Halls with ninety-one votes, the individual pork pie got eighty-seven, Fabio twenty-seven, and Terry's testicles got one vote.

At dinner Hannah was sitting on her own. I asked her to come and join us and she did! Wow, eh? I was a bit nervous. I have this strange feeling we ought to be friends. Natalia talked to me about going out with Mike Ticknell. I wish she hadn't, but I hope Hannah was jealous.

8pm met Mike outside the main building. I was wearing my short black skirt, open-necked white blouse, black jacket. We went into town for a drink. I had two tomato juices. He paid. I like that. We talked till 10:30pm. He walked me back. He gave me a peck on the lips. I really like that. How sweet.

Friday 24th February 1989, University

Worked in The Halls bar. Spud, as always, bought me a drink. Spud is overweight, with a greasy black ponytail and round glasses. He always wears a waistcoat.

I was talking to Charlie the skinhead for a long time. He was telling me about how he got into fights in pubs. He does look like a bit of a thug. He said that people just come up and hit you. I didn't believe him, so he said he'd take me round the roughest pubs in town so I could see. We agreed Thursday.

Monday 27th February 1989, University

Took the polyester and my Miss Williams photo to the print shop. It cost me £80.50. The printed material will be ready next week.

I had always thought that Roberta was pretty, but it occurred to me tonight that she is *gorgeous*.

Tuesday 28th February 1989, University

Played on Luigi, the Italian department computer. Typed in my name as 'Miss Williams' again. On the door was a typed list of people who'd used Luigi recently, and 'Miss Williams' was on it. Mrs. Deverson must have seen. It's so funny.

5:45pm Hannah came to see me (!). She said that the Christian Union were holding discussion meetings every Thursday and they were telling everyone who seemed interested. ...

Saw Roberta in the bar. She is so incredibly attractive. God, she's gorgeous.

Wednesday 1st March 1989, University

Worked in The Halls bar with Spud. He walked me back and taught me to play *Back In The USSR* in the piano room.

Thursday 2nd March 1989, University

Card from Mr. McKay with 'Thank you' on the front. I was so happy. He thanked me for the birthday present (a silk tie) and card and told me to forget about school.

7:30pm went to the Christian discussion group. Hannah wasn't there! Three people were leading it. And I was the only one who turned up.

Met Charlie 8pm. He said there was a change of plan. Six of us went to the local pub instead. Such a disappointment.

11:20pm talked to Natalia in her room for two hours about a boy she likes. She said she couldn't imagine going out with a girl or kissing a girl. She said that two people the same would be dull.

Friday 3rd March 1989, University > Home

4:15pm after French literature, I came out of the lecture room and for some reason I turned sharply round. I was starring straight into the eyes of the lesbian girl.

Got home 9:30pm as a surprise for Mother's Day. Mum looked so happy. She hugged me.

Sunday 5th March 1989, Home > University

Louise, Nigel, and Sophie came round for Mother's Day.

Dad drove me to the station. I asked him about the letter I'd had from Grandma not knowing about Louise's baby. He said he wasn't going to mention it to me, but as I'd brought the matter up, Grandma had phoned Dad and so he had had to tell her. He said that Mum and Dad had agreed not to tell anyone as they were ashamed. Grandma had understood.

Monday 6th March 1989, University

I was practising my German oral contribution on floor eleven before going into the class. Mr. Greaves walked past. "... Natasha, I didn't recognise you without your Walkman on."

It's Lesbian and Gay Men Awareness Week. In the middle of the Students' Union Monday market was the Lesbian and Gay Society stall. The lesbian girl was there. ... She's so sweet. Wow! I bought a copy of Gay Times (£1.20). I just wanted to burst out laughing.

2:15pm the lesbian girl went up on the paternoster as I was standing on floor eleven. Our eyes met again. I love that.

Went to the print shop to fetch the Miss Williams material. It was wrong. They'd printed it up-down-up-down, and I'd wanted it up-up-up-up. They would print it again.

More hustings for posts on The Halls committee. Terry (not his testicles) was standing for secretary. They were making jokes about Miss Chappel. Terry said he got his accommodation bill for this term and was so annoyed with it that he attacked it with his compass and Miss Chappel said to him, "Are you telling me to fuck off?"

Tuesday 7th March 1989, University

There was a speech by a gay vicar at 2pm in the Students' Union TV room. I plucked up enough courage to go. I was the first to arrive. I talked for a couple of minutes with the vicar. Then the lesbian walked in, with an older woman. The latter said to him: "I'm Vikki's mum."

The lesbian is called Vikki!

More people arrived. We sat round in a circle. "Vikki" was looking at me all the time, which was pretty embarrassing. Every time I looked up, she was looking at me. The vicar spoke, followed by a discussion. I sat looking at the ceiling.

I had to leave 3:25pm as I was late for French conversation.

The Halls Ball tonight. Natalia didn't want to come. I was really disappointed about that. I wore my white dress and black jacket. Gabrielle and I went about 10pm. I had two pints of lager and a Baileys. We stayed in the bar and talked to people. I was getting drunk.

11pm-12pm I had to work in the top bar with Guy Gilpin. I managed very well in my condition. I had to concentrate hard to add up the prices though.

Afterwards I found Gabrielle. We stood talking to people in the foyer. I kept taking bits of people's drinks. Guy Gilpin came up. I put my arm around him and rested my head on his shoulder. I could see Spud out of the corner of my eye, looking at me the whole time. He seemed jealous. After a while he came over. Guy passed me to him.

I said to Spud, "Let's go into the bar and finish up all the left-over drinks."

We found about half a pint each and drank them. I felt decidedly ill and had to stay sitting for a bit. Then I pulled Spud up and said, "Let's dance." I couldn't stand upright very well, so we danced hugging. It was very nice. Then we kissed for a while. I absolutely love kissing so much. I could do it forever.

The ball finished at 1am. Spud and I sat down. A few other people were still there. I suddenly felt awful and was sick all over the floor. Spud said, "Come on, we'd better get you back to the house."

When we got in, Carol asked him, "Do you want any help?" He said "No," but she came anyway. They sat me down on my bed and made me drink a pint of water. Some other people wandered in and out. Carol was lovely. She kept looking questioningly up at the Miss Williams photos on my wall.

I said, "She's very pretty, isn't she?"

Carol said, "Yes, she is actually."

"Don't you think she's beautiful?"

"Yes. Who is she?"

"My French teacher."

Spud left. Carol undressed me and put me to bed. I fell straight to sleep.

Wednesday 8th March 1989, University

I felt rather ill this morning. 10:30am I went to the Italian secretary to ask her for an Aspirin. I noticed on top of her rack of things to do, a sheet of paper with the word 'Natasha' in large, blue handwriting. I tried to read some without the secretary noticing. It said ...

> *Natasha is not technically an offender. She attends regularly and works well.*

My heart was beating really fast. Could it be me? It must be. This was to be typed up and put in my file? What have I done? The Miss Williams photocopies? Typing Miss Williams's name into Luigi? What? I felt victimised.

I went back to the secretary's office at 11:30am to get another Aspirin, but the sheet had gone.

Played on Luigi. Typed in 'Williams' plus her initials several times. Then decided to type in her full name. I tried doing this a number of times. The computer responded with ...

'That doesn't sound like a name to me' ... 'That's not acceptable' ... 'And my name's Garibaldi.'

I was so shocked. I typed in random names and letters. They were accepted. I tried her first name and middle name. Not accepted. I typed in, 'What's your problem' for my first name and 'Eh' for my surname. That was accepted. I typed in, 'What a stupid machine you are' as first name and variations on her first name and middle name for surname. That was accepted. I typed in 'Ner ner ner ner ner.'

Then I got scared. I might get into a lot of trouble.

Letter from Mum. Emily's mum had rung her. She's offered me a job for the Easter holidays. As Emily has injured her back roller-skating, she hasn't been going to school. She'd like me to go to their house over the holidays as company for Emily and to help her catch up with her languages. I was so excited and happy that I screamed. And Emily will probably tell Miss Williams. I'll have to make sure her German is excellent.

7pm rang Emily's mum. She was delighted that I would love the job. She kept saying it was such a load off her mind. She asked if

£15 a day was alright. Wow, yes. We agreed Monday to Thursday. The teachers at school and Miss Byron will get to know about it.

9:15pm Spud came to see me. We went to the bar and sat talking to some people until about 10:30pm. He invited himself back to my room for twenty minutes. On leaving he pecked me on the lips and said, "I've been plucking up courage to do that for hours."

Monday 13th March 1989, University

Today was the first day I'd ever been to the uni without concealer stick on. My skin was getting too dry.

Tuesday 14th March 1989, University

My period started. Tomorrow I was planning to have my vagina pierced. Annoying.

12:05pm appointment with the head of German to talk about how I was getting on. I assured her that all was fine. She asked me what I wanted to do as a job. I told her I wanted to teach at my old school.

"Is that because of anything in particular, like the teacher you told me about who came here?" (I didn't remember telling her that.)

"Yes."

"Why does it have to be the same school?"

"I want to be with her."

In general, she said things like, "You're very committed" and "You don't ever seem to worry." She said that I ought to worry because you do things better then. I disagreed.

Picked up the material from the print shop. They gave me the one they got wrong as well, so I've got two lots. Brilliant.

Waiting to go to French conversation I saw Mr. Wolfe's face. He's so beautiful.

Letter from Grandma (Dad's mum). She told me never to be so foolish as to do what Louise has done. I didn't like her attitude.

Gabrielle and I went to Spud's party in his room. They were saying that application forms for halls of residence had been out for ages and had to be in on Friday and that the house that Miss Williams lived in may not be available. Shit.

Wednesday 15th March 1989, University

9:05am went to Miss Chappel to get an accommodation form for next year. It's an uncomfortable situation as we both know what each other is thinking. I put Miss Williams's old room as my first choice.

In the Frederick Building loos there is anti and pro lesbian writing on the wall. I added in pencil a lesbian symbol (two women's signs) with sun rays round the outside. I wonder if anyone will write any comments?

Thursday 16th March 1989, University

Eight out of fifteen of us turned up to French language, so Mr. Martin took us all to one of the bars in the Students' Union and bought a few of us a drink. What a sweetie.

Friday 17th March 1989, University > Home

In the Frederick Building loos where I had drawn the lesbian symbol there is now an arrow pointing at it with the words, *Thank you sister!* I thought that was hilarious and brilliant. I felt wanted and warm.

Dad came to fetch me. Got home about 8:30pm. Janusz rang to ask me if I'd go out with him one evening. I said I would.

Saturday 18th March 1989, Home

Bought four metres of 100% polyester (£11.80). Bought purple and red dye. Dyed one of the pieces of polyester purple.

Sunday 19th March 1989, Home

8:30pm Emily's mum came to fetch me.

Emily was lying on the sofa in the living room. Miss Byron has been to see her in hospital. Some teachers have sent cards or phoned. Miss Williams hasn't done anything. Maybe it's because I'm her friend?

Emily's friends say Miss Williams is not wearing an engagement ring.

Tested Emily on her German vocab. We stayed up till 3:10am.

Monday 20th March 1989, Home

11:10am rang the school secretary to make an appointment with Miss Byron. ... Am I mad?

She asked, "What's it about?"

"It's an apology."

Emily and I spent the day watching the TV and doing German.

Phoned Sara. She's ever so pleased to be making the shirts for me. We arranged to meet Tuesday 28th to go for a drink in the Vaults.

8:23pm Janusz phoned. I missed the end of *Brookside*.

Tuesday 21st March 1989, Home

2:35pm started out for school. Bit nervous, but really wanted to do it. When I knocked on the office door there were two secretaries, Miss Tennyson, and Miss Byron in there (Help!). Miss Byron came out. Miss Tennyson said "Hello" and smiled (phew ...). I said "Hello" back, and followed Miss Byron to her room. She made a comment about the weather.

She didn't sit at her desk, which I thought was nice of her. We sat on comfy chairs at a coffee table.

"What was it you wanted to talk to me about?"

"I have to make an apology that I should have made a long time ago. ... Do you know what for?"

"I have a fair idea."

"The evening of the Christmas Fair ..."

"You did the writing on the wall."

I nodded.

"Were you responsible for the other writing?"

I said I wasn't. I asked her how they realised it was me. She said they weren't completely sure, but put two and two together, and that I had been at the Christmas Fair anyway. She said, "It must have taken a lot of courage to come and say this."

I offered to pay for the damage.

She said there wasn't any. The caretaker got it off. I could buy him a box of chocolates.

I will.

"The wall isn't the important thing, it's the person, the fact that you felt uptight enough to do it."

The words I wrote were not mentioned, neither was Miss Williams's name.

Miss Byron said I needed to channel my feelings into "like and respect," to concentrate on people my own age (That hurt. It made Miss Williams seem unattainable), and to get more involved in other things.

"What did she say?"

"I haven't discussed it with her."

She said she was delighted that I had come to apologise and it would all be forgotten. I felt so happy. She added, "Obviously I would have preferred that it hadn't happened. You won't do it again, will you?"

"Never."

She asked me how I was getting on at university. She said she hoped she'd see me at School Reunion in the summer. I said I'd be there.

I felt so happy and relieved as I walked back to Emily's.

Thursday 23rd March 1989, Home

Last night I had an incredible dream: I was lying on a row of comfy chairs in The Halls bar. Miss Williams was sitting by my head, rubbing cream on her arm. I looked up. She had her left breast exposed. I could see faint blue veins. She lay down beside me with her back turned. I acted hurt and made as if to turn my back too, but turned full-circle instead. She rolled her eyes and tutted. I took her wrist to look at. She pulled it away. I was acting as if drunk. She said she was going. I got up as well. I offered to buy her a drink in The Halls bar. She refused. I had my right arm round her waist. My left arm was holding her right arm in front of us.

We were outside now. I asked if she wanted to see my room. She seemed interested. We were walking beside a flowerbed. I moved to kiss her. The kiss landed half on her lips, half on her cheek. She swung me round and in a matter-of-fact voice she said, "Sick."

I said, "I didn't do that."

She said, "Yes, you did."

"I'm telling you I didn't. ... I did *this*." And I kissed her on the left cheek.

Then Emily knocked on the door and woke me up (grrr).

Emily's dad drove me home about 5pm. Her parents are jewellers. I asked him how much he'd charge me to make a bracelet like my silver one in eighteen carat gold (for Miss Williams's birthday present). He said just under £400. He'd make it for me trade price, not retail.

Friday 24th March 1989, Home

Bought three metres of cotton and *Dancerama* by Sigue Sigue Sputnik.

Decided to get 'I LOVE MISS WILLIAMS' tattooed across the back of my left hand.

Song For Europe tonight. They were all rubbish.

Saturday 25th March 1989, Home

First day back at McDonald's. Janusz asked me to the cinema on Thursday. I accepted.

A very nice Pakistani chap called Massoud was working this evening. He kept asking me to marry him. When we were alone in the back room together, he kept kissing me and pinching my bum. He would pounce on me and stick his tongue into my mouth. He asked me for my address and phone number. I gave them to him. He said the most beautiful things. It was very flattering, but extremely weird.

Cathy was asking about my tattoo: "Friendly love or *in* love?" She said that it's '*in* love' if your heart skips a beat when you see her. I'd never thought of that before. My heart *stops* when I see her.

Monday 27th March 1989, Home

Sore throat. Wrote off to agencies for *au pair* jobs in Italy and Germany.

Tuesday 28th March 1989, Home

Met Sara in the Vaults. We had a vodka and Coke (yuck). She asked to see my tattoo. She said she'd thought it would be a lot bigger. That upset me.

I hadn't told her what I wanted her to make my shirts out of. I showed her the Miss Williams material. She thought it was brilliant. We discussed designs. I ordered two shirts and a waistcoat from her (£10 per item). She said they're probably the most original items she'll ever make.

Wednesday 29th March 1989, Home

Spent eight or nine hours going through German with Emily. We did twelve chapters. I hope Miss Williams is pleased.

Thursday 30th March 1989, Home

Emily's dad drove me home for 5:30pm. Apparently Massoud had phoned up yesterday and the day before. He phoned 7:49pm this evening. He made me promise to meet him outside McDonald's at 8:45am tomorrow.

Janusz came to pick me up at 8pm. We went to a pub. Had half a lager. Then to another pub. Had half a lager. Then to the cinema to see *Naked Gun*. Pretty funny.

We got home 11:35pm. Janusz kept talking till 11:54pm, parked outside our house like he didn't know what else to do. Then he said it was getting late, and started up the engine.

"Aren't you going to walk me to the door, then?" I wasn't going to waste four hours without a kiss.

Kissing is my second favourite occupation in the world.

Third is listening to my favourite music.

First is looking at Miss Williams.

It was about the worst kiss I've ever had.

Friday 31st March 1989, Home

Met Massoud outside McDonald's at 8:45am. We went to the Wimpy. He bought me an orange juice. He asked me to skip work and come out with him instead.

Started McDonald's shift 9:30am. It was tedious. Everyone was talking about Massoud and me. And so many 'lez' comments about my tattoo.

I asked one of the Lower Sixth who works in McDonald's for the name of someone in her year who does German. She gave me a name and I phoned the girl up when I got home. My plan was to offer her £1 for each photo plus negative of Miss Williams that she would take on the German trip. Before I told her what I wanted her to do, she informed me that Miss Williams didn't want to go on the trip this year.

8pm Janusz rang for a chat.

Saturday 1st April 1989, Home

Bought three metres of cotton. Photocopied Miss Williams's signature for a design I'm working on.

Tuesday 4th April 1989, Home

We got two chapters ahead of what Emily's class has done. I hope Miss Williams is impressed.

Thursday 6th April 1989, Home

Dyed two metres of polyester red.

McDonald's shift 7pm. Janusz invited me to a fancy dress party for Saturday.

Saturday 8th April 1989, Home

9:30pm Janusz picked me up for the fancy dress party. We went as Laurel and Hardy. He drove me home 11:20pm because I wanted to finish my Miss Williams design. He walked me to the door again. The kiss wasn't as bad this time, but not good.

Monday 10th April 1989, Home

Emily's dad told me he'd worked out how much the gold bracelet's going to cost. It will be 1.3 millimetres thick and eighteen carat gold ... so £575. ... This is the trade price. If I were buying retail, it would cost £800. They are going to let me pay it in instalments.

Friday 14th April 1989, Home

Sitting in the living room with Mum, Louise, and Sophie, Mum said to me, "Is that a real tattoo or do you write it on every morning?" I thought she knew. I said, "It's a tattoo." She looked quite shocked and upset. She asked where I'd got it done and how much it cost. Louise kept trying to change the subject.

Saturday 15th April 1989, Home
Bought Dairy Box chocolates for the school caretaker.

Tuesday 18th April 1989, Home
Emily's friend Kim came round after school. Without my saying anything at all, Kim told me what Miss Williams was wearing ... (black shoes, white tights, black skirt, white blouse, royal blue cardigan). She had taken note of this because I always ask her.

Wednesday 19th April 1989, Home
Last day at Emily's. Kim came after school. Again without my asking she told me what Miss Williams was wearing (black patent shoes with gold chains on the front, dark blue tights, dark blue open-necked dress).

Emily's mum drove me home. We had a brilliant conversation about interviewing people, during which she said she *always* checked references thoroughly. She'd checked up on me by phoning school. She wouldn't tell me who she'd spoken to. She said, "Someone there thinks very highly of you."

"Was it Miss Byron?"

"No."

"Mr. McKay?"

"No."

"Miss Williams?" (!)

"No."

It was driving me crazy, but she wouldn't tell me.

"Why did you check up?"

"You could have run up an enormous phone bill, had friends over, not done what you were there for. Things could have gone missing."

Sunday 23rd April 1989, Home > University

Last day of the holidays. I wish I could just stay at home.

Sara phoned 2:30pm, said she'd spilled coffee on my Miss Williams shirt. ...

... She was joking.

I went over to hers on the way back to uni. The first Miss Williams shirt and the waistcoat were ready. I tried them on. They're incredible.

Sara's younger brother takes vacuum cleaners apart as a hobby. I said, "You're brother's a bit eccentric, isn't he?"

She said, "You can bloody talk."

At the station I scratched 'I love Miss Williams' into one of the waiting room benches on platform two. Caught the 5:41pm train.

Natalia didn't get back till 10pm. She came straight to my room. I was so glad to see her. Her voice is so different from other people's. I'd missed her a lot.

Monday 24th April 1989, University

Went to the print shop. Ordered:

- photo of Miss Williams printed as a pattern on the purple dyed polyester
- Miss Williams's full name printed as a pattern on the red dyed polyester
- a white T-shirt with a photo of Miss Williams printed on the front

Altogether it cost £135.

As I was doing my Italian homework this evening, I kept wishing Vikki was here. It must be so nice and gentle to kiss a girl.

Tuesday 25th April 1989, University

Book sale in the Students' Union. Thought I'd go in because Vikki the lesbian might be in there. She wasn't. ... But I saw her go in an hour later. Followed her. Stood at a table, pretending to be engrossed in a book. She was working her way towards me. I felt like I loved her. My heart was beating really fast. She got near me ... but then one of her friends (another lesbian) came over to talk to her. I love Vikki's voice.

After French conversation, saw Vikki at the pigeonholes. I walked past her into the cloakroom, but when I came out, she was gone. In the loos where I wrote the lesbian symbol last term, someone had added:

Fucking benders everywhere you go—Yuck.

I thought that was very funny.

Wednesday 26th April 1989, University

Didn't see my darling Vikki today.

Designed personalised writing paper: Miss Williams collage.

Pinned a photocopy of Miss Williams's photo on the notice board outside the Students' Union newspaper office.

Friday 28th April 1989, University

We learn next year's accommodation today. I was really excited, but didn't go and look in my pigeonhole. Went into town instead. When I got back it was dinnertime. I got the letter from my pigeonhole and stood in the queue, got dinner, sat down, still without opening it, but then couldn't wait. I got it!! I'm going to live in Miss Williams's old room next year. I was thrilled. Natalia told me I blushed. I was just so happy. It's amazing.

Tuesday 2nd May 1989, University

Wore my Miss Williams waistcoat for the first time today. Tonya said she recognised the face and that it was really good. Other people asked who she was, and praised it. But most people didn't say anything.

Stuck Miss Williams photocopies on the backs of the benches in the main hall balcony in the Students' Union.

Wednesday 3rd May 1989, University

In the Frederick Building loos where I wrote the lesbian symbol, there have been lots of comments. Noticed today that all the defensive comments are in the same handwriting. That made me laugh. That wall is covered in graffiti, but the opposite wall is blank, so I wrote: *What's wrong with* this *wall?* and drew another lesbian symbol with hearts all around.

This evening there was a knock at the door. I opened up, and there stood ... Hannah. What amazingly beautiful light brown eyes. What a lovely surprise. She'd come to invite me to a Christian Union meeting on Friday.

I said, "I'd like to introduce you to the former occupant of your room."

She didn't say much about it.

Friday 5th May 1989, University

Went to the Christian Union meeting that Hannah invited me to. Hannah was leading it, so I could just sit and look at her. Have I mentioned her eyes?

Saturday 6th May 1989, University

Went to The Halls disco. I was dancing with Ewan. At one point he went off and got himself a drink, but didn't offer me one. That does not impress me at all, but I wanted a kiss. His kiss wasn't excellent, but he certainly tried hard. His hands were up and down my back. He was kissing my neck—which I loved, and nibbling my ear—very nice. But I didn't enjoy the kiss. This time I remembered to imagine it was Miss Williams, but with his stubble, height, size, and sweat it didn't really work. He tried to invite himself back to my room for a coffee, but didn't succeed.

Yugoslavia won the Eurovision Song Contest.

Monday 8th May 1989, University

Today it struck me that there's such an easy way to get to know Vikki and I'd never thought of it before: Go to one of the Lesbian and Gay Society meetings! So simple. I think I shall go on 5th June once most of my exams are over. I can't wait.

Tuesday 9th May 1989, University

Mock French oral. While I was sitting outside the room, reading the passage, Mr. Greaves walked passed. He said, "Batteries run down?"

After dinner I went to Natalia's room to tell her something that had been worrying me for a few days: "Sometimes I just like you and sometimes I think I really love you and I don't know how I'm going to cope when you're not here next year."

She said, "Wow."

Thursday 11th May 1989, University

Went to the book sale in the Students' Union. Vikki was there. She always is! We were going round the hall in opposite directions, and for a while we were standing right next to each other. I was so nervous. I pretended to read a book. I'm sure she's thinking the same as me. I bought *Claudine Married* by Collette.

Read *Claudine Married* to page 108.

Friday 12th May 1989, University

Bought forty-eight packets of crisps.

Sunday 14th May 1989, University

Annual photo of all residents of The Halls today. I wore my Miss
Williams waistcoat.

Tuesday 16th May 1989, University

Visited Natalia. We were talking about babies. I spoke as I have
before about who I want to be the father of my baby. I never let on
who it is. This really annoys her. So, this time she locked her door
and wouldn't let me go until I told her.

I said, "If you really thought about it, you could work it out."

"Sigue Sigue Sputnik?"

"No."

"Bono?" (I never stop listening to my *Unforgettable Fire* LP
by U2)

"No."

"Miss Williams's boyfriend?"

"I don't think she has one. Do you think I'd take someone
away from her?"

"Miss Williams's father?"

"No."

"Is he related to her?"

I just kept looking at her.

"Obviously he is. ... Miss Williams's brother?"

"Yes."

She said that was interesting and she never would have
thought of that. This made me very happy.

Wednesday 17th May 1989, University

At breakfast Gabrielle said, "You can define Natasha in one word: *obstinacy*."

Thursday 18th May 1989, University

Graffiti in the library:

> *It really turns me on to see dogs shitting. It makes me want to screw their dirty bums.*

Can you believe that? That's so disgusting. I love it.

Saturday 20th May 1989, University

This evening I was looking a lot at the first photo of Miss Williams that Michelle took for me. It was upsetting me that she seemed to only look like her in that photo, and that she looked very different in my posters of her. It seemed like the person I've got all over my wall isn't her at all. It felt like everything I'm doing in my whole life is pointless.

I had a strange feeling that I want to sleep with someone. Who?—Anthony Hill, or anyone really.

But also I want the first one to be someone special.

About 10:30pm I suggested to Gabrielle that we go to The Halls bar. Anthony Hill was there. We sat quite near him. Spud joined us. We got into conversation with Anthony, but then he left. If he'd invited me to his room, I would have said yes.

Spud walked back with us. As he turned off towards his room, he kissed his fist and put it up to my cheek.

Tuesday 23rd May 1989, University

Phone call from the volunteering organisation about working in Germany this summer. I got my third choice: renovating an old theatre.

Thursday 25th May 1989, University

My most dreaded exam today: German literature. I took a photo of Miss Williams in with me. The head of German was invigilating. I had the photo on my desk.

Went to the bar. Anthony Hill came over for a chat. I asked to borrow his Italian notes, so we went back to his room. We talked, smoked, listened to music. I told him Gabrielle had said he looked romantic, so he came back with me to meet her. I was not flattered. Anthony and I played darts in my room. Gabrielle came in. We all went to her room. We talked for a bit. Then I left them together.

Saturday 27th May 1989, University

Natalia and Gabrielle had their last exam this afternoon. To celebrate, they threw a party in the piano room. I went down about 10:30pm. There weren't many there at that time—about ten people sitting on the floor, drinking gin. I had some. It was disgusting. So, I started on the wine as I was determined to get drunk.

More people started to arrive. I was feeling increasingly wobbly.

Natalia rarely drinks, but got extremely drunk this evening and retired to her room.

Gabrielle fetched some people from the bar. I was drinking from the bottle by this point. I was nearly falling over, so one of the French girls and Brandon (an American bloke in The Halls) helped me to a seat.

Brandon stayed with me, and we kissed a lot. I wasn't terribly conscious. He asked me, "Where's your room?" I ignored him and carried on kissing.

Anthony and Brandon took me up to my room and laid me on my bed. Anthony left. Brandon was kissing me. I was wearing leggings. His right hand was gliding lightly over my crotch. It tickled. He slipped his hand down my knickers and rubbed slightly backwards and forwards. I wished he'd slip his finger in. But I didn't have the energy to tell him. It didn't excite me, it was just … nice.

I was not very conscious, but I half realised that my leggings and knickers were being pulled down. I saw vaguely that he had taken his trousers down as well, and was moving down on top of me. I was sort of intrigued and curious as to what it might be like. But I also thought "Oh shit" and definitely didn't want it to happen.

I felt a bit trapped and had to get out of it.

I was so drunk that I couldn't speak. And I could barely move. It took some effort to summon enough energy to roll out from under him and fall onto the floor.

Phew.

I want the first to be someone special (Miss Williams's brother, Mr. McKay, Mr. Wolfe, another uni teacher, someone famous, or someone I love).

Brandon pulled my clothes up and put me back on the bed. I think he made sure I was OK. Then he left. I was sick. Twice. Then fell asleep. This must have been about midnight.

About 12:30am Gabrielle and Anthony came in to check up on me, waking me up. I felt more ill than I ever have. I was shivering, and my stomach hurt so much. They fetched me water, got me blankets, held my hand in turns. They left and I fell back to sleep.

Sunday 28th May 1989, University

Woke up about 6:30am. ... Ouch. What incredible pain. I couldn't move. Why don't I learn?

I was thinking that I didn't like the fact that I wasn't excited by the finger. I never get excited by kissing either (except just a tiny bit with Ian Ashcroft). Why is this?

Gabrielle came in to see if I was alright. She gave me a pain-killer. It didn't help at all. I heard Anthony's voice. He'd been with Gabrielle all night.

I lay in bed, as still as I could, till lunchtime. Walked over with Gabrielle and Anthony—slowly. Ate lunch—slowly. I heard that Brandon was in a worse state. He couldn't even make it to lunch.

When I got back, I lay down again.

Got up for dinner. Felt very nearly well. It was beautiful. Gabrielle went over to sit with Anthony, who was sitting with Brandon. I was really annoyed with her, but I suppose it's better to get it over and done with. I said to him, "I heard you weren't doing too well?" And made a couple of other comments.

Cleaned up the sick by (and on) my bed. Had to put the bedspread and a blanket in the bath, they were so disgusting.

Have done absolutely nothing constructive all day.

Monday 29th May 1989, University

I can't get rid of the smell!

Tuesday 30th May 1989, University

Bought *Storms In Africa* by Enya, The theme to *Prisoner Cell Block H* by Lynne Hamilton, and *If You Don't Know Me By Now* by Simply Red.

Had to hand in a form to the Italian secretary. Mrs. Deverson (Just look at those eyes) was just coming out. She glared at me as usual.

The smell of sick is worse than ever.

Friday 2nd June 1989, University

Italian literature exam. I was ecstatic when it was over.

At dinner I went over to Roberta to ask her about being able to come back to The Halls early next term. I just sat there and looked at her eyes. She's a painting.

Monday 5th June 1989, University

Worked up the courage to go to my first Lesbian and Gay Society meeting, 6pm in the Students' Union TV room. ... Arrived to find no-one there. ...

So looking forward to tomorrow—my last written exam. Freedom. Then just Italian oral to go.

Tuesday 6th June 1989, University

Went into a newsagent's and looked through a magazine of naked men. I've come to the conclusion that penises are ugly.

7:25pm went to visit Hannah to invite her to the cinema to see *The Blob*—the best choice of a bad lot. She sounded hesitant, even more so when I explained what the film was about. She said no. I was talking to her for thirteen minutes. She invited me to a Christian Union barbecue.

I decided instead to go and ask Spud. He has an exam (a what?) first thing tomorrow. He said yes.

The film was a bit scary. I had to look away quite a lot. We went to a pub afterwards. Spud bought me a tomato juice. He invited me back to his room. He played me some music on his guitar.

About 12:30am I said I should be getting back. He walked me. He asked, "Do I get a goodnight kiss?" I kissed him for about a second on the lips.

Thursday 8th June 1989, University

Bought hazel hair dye mousse. It's a disguise for the school Open Day. That hurt as I wrote it.

Decided I really wanted some condoms—just in case. ... Bought a packet of three Mates (59p).

Friday 9th June 1989, University

Started my design for the wrapping paper for Miss Williams's birthday present.

Today I put my first ever light bulb in.

Met Spud at the Phoenix Theatre 10:45pm. He bought me an orange juice and lemonade. We saw a certificate 18 film, pretty erotic in parts and rather good. I thought it was beautiful when one of the characters said that it's being inside the woman he loves that makes him come.

And I thought I can never be inside her.

Spud invited me back to his room to listen to records. He walked me back. A couple of pecks on the lips and a hug.

Cooked some noodles in the kitchen. The ex-president of the Students' Union was in there. I put an Oxo cube and some tomato relish in with the noodles. He was horrified, said he would send me some recipes.

Wednesday 14th June 1989, University

Bought *Prisoner Cell Block H* theme for Natalia as a going away present. She loves it and keeps playing mine.

Bought black sunglasses to wear at the school Open Day if I go.

Went into The Jeans Company. Got talking to an assistant called Larry. He saw my tattoo and asked me if I was gay. I have never answered that question. He told me he was.

I asked him if a woman were to proposition him, would he accept? He thought it was funny. He hesitated, "... It depends. ... As an experience." He's never been with a girl.

When I left, he said, "Aren't you going to proposition me, then?"

It was tempting. I *love* gay men. What a turn-on.

Thursday 15th June 1989, University

Gabrielle's last day in The Halls. It wasn't sad because it doesn't seem real that she won't be in her room anymore.

8pm I went to visit Ian Ashcroft. I wanted him to kiss me because, although his kiss doesn't seem very good and it leaves half your face wet, he's the only one to ever excite me a bit.

Was informed that Ian had gone home and wasn't coming back till Tuesday.

Natalia came up to my room. She was being mentally tormented by the fact that her friend, who she had just been out with, had tried to kiss her. He has ruined their friendship.

Friday 16th June 1989, University

Went to Ysabel's office. Took two photos of her. She invited me over to her room for whenever I like, to see her photographs. It's her hobby, she told me. She loves it.

Saturday 17th June 1989, University

Went to visit Ysabel to look at her photographs. She wasn't in. I looked for her in the bar. There was a party going on. Mr. Martin was there. I want to sleep with someone important first. Why doesn't he ask me?

Natalia gave me a present—a tin of tuna—because whenever she has it for her tea I ask her for some.

Sunday 18th June 1989, University

8am Natalia knocked on my door to say goodbye. She wanted it to be quick. She hates goodbyes. She told me to stay in bed. I got out. I gave her a package in which I'd put the theme to *Prisoner Cell Block H* and a photo of Miss Williams. She kissed me on the cheek, then made for the door.

I felt overwhelmed. "Don't go."

She said, "Bye Natasha" and left.

I followed her a short way. "Natalia, come back."

She carried on walking. I just burst into tears. I cried and cried on the bed. Really surprised myself.

Monday 19th June 1989, University

9:20pm visited Ysabel to see her photographs. She seemed pleased enough to see me. Beautiful room. I chose *Rattle and Hum* by U2 from her collection.

She asked me to psycho-analyse her. I said that her being so outgoing suggested insecurity. She replied that she was shy. I added that she appears to do what she wants without caring about people's opinion of her, yet that in itself is an image that she tries to portray—so she does care. I was making it up, just trying to impress her.

I told her I prefer being on my own. She'd heard that. Some students who didn't realise that she knew me had told her that I was a bit of a loner.

She offered to buy me a drink. "What do you want?"

"You decide."

She came back with two pints of Carlsberg.

She showed me her photos. They're not bad. One of them looked like crosses. So, we were talking about religion. She told me she's a strict atheist. I said I'd guessed this from remarks she'd made.

"Are *you* religious?" she asked.

"No."

"I didn't think so."

"Why not?"

She was reluctant to tell me why she didn't think I was religious.

I insisted.

"You wouldn't be wearing that T-shirt if you were."

I was wearing my red T-shirt with a print of Miss Williams on both sides. I was surprised. I asked her to explain.

"You know what I'm talking about."

I insisted.

"People talk. Things are said."

At this point there was a knock on the door (argh). Two blokes came in, friends of Ysabel's. I was annoyed. I wished they'd go. They didn't.

Tuesday 20th June 1989, University

To the Frederick Building 10:35am, forgetting that the results weren't out till noon. Talked to Roberta for half an hour. She told me about a lesbian couple who were teachers at the school she went to, for some reason.

Went to get my French results. Saw Mr. Martin. I wasn't nervous, I just violently wanted to do well. He was very pleased with me. I got a 2:1. Thrilled. He said my language paper was excellent, the best in the class.

A student came running up, shouting, "Everyone in first year has passed their German." I felt great. Mr. Greaves said, "Come in, Natasha. Take a seat." He was looking happy. I got a 2:2. People did worse than me on the language paper. He said I'd done a lot better than they'd expected.

"Have you enjoyed this year?"

"I've absolutely loved it. It's been great."

"I look forward to seeing your smiling face and your Walkman next year."

My Italian tutors were very pleased with my Italian result. I got a 2:1 overall. I got a good first for my language paper (not just an average first).

Over the moon with my results because now I'm equal to Miss Williams (or better, because I didn't have German A Level).

Wednesday 21st June 1989, University

Tidied my room brilliantly, just in case I can catch Mr. Martin or any teacher who decides to come to The Halls Ball tonight.

There was a bouncy castle outside, and a steel band in the bar. I sat in the bar and listened. The singer said that everyone sitting down had to come and dance. Most got up. I stayed sitting. Rocky, who I only know to smile to, came over to me: "Are you coming, or am I going to carry you?" I said no. So, he picked me up and carried me over to where they were dancing. That is just so nice. For a second I loved him.

Talked to Spud for half an hour. Worked the bar with Ewan. Had half a pint of lager—all I had to drink all night.

Into the disco in the dining room to try and find someone for a good kiss. Roberta looked beautiful. I sat on one of the tables, watching everyone. It looked like Charlie the skinhead was hanging around. He came over to me, said let's go out and talk. We went into the bar. He said I was being cool. He moved in towards me and we kissed.

We were right in the middle of the bar. His friends were making comments from either side. He told me I was a good kisser.

Spud came up. I hadn't realised he was in the bar. He started talking to me while I was sitting on Charlie's knee. I felt a bit bad.

Charlie asked me to go back to his room with him. I wasn't sure. I didn't want to sleep with him, but I didn't mind it going further than kissing, so I agreed.

We got to his room 12:25am. He sat down on the bed, took my hand and pulled me down. We started kissing. He bent down over me so we were lying on the bed. He unbuttoned the front of my dress. He lifted up my bra cup and was kissing my right breast. It wasn't exciting.

He rubbed outside my knickers, and after a while he slipped his hand down my knickers and started rubbing very firmly backwards and forwards, and up. I love that, except that it was too hard and it hurt. I had to tell him to be gentle. It was nice, but still not exciting. Why?!

We were doing the finger-vagina bit for ages. It really hurt sometimes. I didn't like it whenever he took his hand out, though.

He kept trying to go further. I kept telling him I wasn't going to sleep with him. So, he said before I went I had to give him a blow job (!!) because I had got him so worked up.

I thought: experience.

I was really curious and in a way, flattered. I said yes, but he'd have to show me what to do. He was so surprised that I'd never given a bloke a blow job before. He unzipped his trousers and said I had to get it out. Wow. I love it. He pulled down his underpants a bit, and I saw what I thought was one of his balls. I reached down and took that. It turned out to be the penis. I took it out. It looked pathetic. All tiny and shrivelled up. Then I realised it wasn't erect. He looked so proud of it.

He said, "Suck my dick" (!). I saw it unfold in front of my eyes. It's very clever, but not very beautiful.

I felt hesitant, but put my mouth down over it. The first taste was disgusting. Really sick. I can only describe it as sweet. But once I'd licked that away, it was alright. I did it like I was kissing and the penis was the tongue. It took ages and ages and ages. It wouldn't come.

At stages, he took my head away and tried to have sex with me, using such phrases as "I'm going to screw you" and "You're kipping with me tonight."

I said no. He said, in frustration, "Well, finish me off, then."

Eventually he came. Halleluiah. It was more of this disgusting stuff flowing into my mouth. I let it dribble back out over his penis. Yuck.

I played with his penis for a bit. It's really interesting the way it works.

I said I was definitely going. Got to the door. He kept kissing me. I said "Thank you for the experience," and left 1:20am.

Thursday 22nd June 1989, University > Home
Got up 6:30am after three and a half hours' sleep. I hadn't seen home for sixty-five days.

At the station I saw one of the Lower Fourths. I asked her if the school magazine had come out yet. It came out today. I looked through it. There was a photo of Miss Williams on page nine. It was beautiful. It looked so like her. I asked her if I could buy the magazine off her, but she wanted it. So, as a joke, I asked her to tear the page out. She did! I gave her my address and told her I would give her £1 for any photo of Miss Williams, with the negative, that she sent me.

Friday 23rd June 1989, Home
Bought *Rattle and Hum* by U2.

Went to the tattoo studio. Saw the same guy who did my tattoo. Wanted my vagina and left nipple pierced. Was really nervous about the pain. I thought I'd better ask for the nipple first. He only had a normal ear-piercing gun, but I really wanted it doing.

Eventually, I plucked up enough courage. He got the gun ready. I lifted up my T-shirt, unhooked my bra, and lifted up my left cup. He tried to get my nipple erect. It wasn't sticking out enough. He put a cold bottle on it. In the end, he had to pinch it. He put the gun up. ... Ouucchh! The actual shot wasn't too bad, but it hurt for ages afterwards.

I said I was thinking of having another one.

"Nipple?"

"No."

"Lip?"

"No."

"... Fanny lip?" (!)

"Yes."

I was very glad he said that. I wouldn't have known what to call it.

He got a bench out. I took off my black denim trousers and my knickers, and lay back on the bench. I had a choice between left or right, inner or outer "lip." I asked for left outer. I had my legs either side of the bench. He asked me to open wider. Another tattooist had to hold my left outer lip while he positioned the gun. I liked the idea of two blokes looking at my vagina, but I didn't find it exciting. I hate this. Why don't I ever get excited?

The actual shot hurt, but then it was completely painless. The piercings cost £5 altogether.

Monday 26th June 1989, Home

Emily and I got up 8:45am to work for her French oral tomorrow. She was absolutely rubbish. By the end, I had managed to drum some basics into her. Emily's parents seemed pretty pleased at her consequent enthusiasm.

Emily's mum drove me back 8:30pm. I asked her what she thought of Miss Williams. She replied that Miss Williams had made such a vivid impression on her that she couldn't remember what she was like.

Tuesday 27th June 1989, Home > University

Today was school Open Day, but I couldn't go as it was raining. I had bought a disguise: brown hair mousse and black sunglasses. I felt I would have stuck out rather more like this, in the pouring rain. I wasn't too sad though. It might all have gone wrong. Ideally I would have seen Miss Williams, fallen even more in love with her, and spent the night with Mr. McKay.

Train back to uni. I wanted to find Mr. Martin (my French language tutor. He's in his late twenties) to ask him if he would sleep with me, because I want the first one to be someone special.

There was a disco in the bar at his halls of residence. I saw a girl from our French language class and asked her where he would be. She said that she had just seen him. She gave me directions to his room. I went up, but hung around plucking up courage for a while before knocking on his door. ...

No answer. ...

Backwards and forwards from the bar to his room, looking for him.

Got talking to someone in the bar. Mr. Martin walked in. He smiled at me. ... He was talking to someone. I waited. He finished his conversation and was about to walk past me.

I said, "Mr. Martin, can I have a word with you, please?"

He put his head towards me to hear what I had to say.

I said, "No. Somewhere else."

This was about 10:25pm. We walked off, and ended up sitting on the stairs in the main building. I'd pretty much rehearsed what I was going to say. It was awful. The words were so cringeworthy.

I said something like, "I wanted to ask you a favour. It's really, really embarrassing. Will you do it?"

His face said 'Oh dear.' I'm sure he knew what I was going to say.

"You'll have to ask me the question first."

I hesitated. I just couldn't pronounce those awful words. Eventually, I said something like, "I have this predicament ... which is ... that (really slowly, then I plucked up so much courage) ... I can't sleep with anyone."

He didn't move. He just sat there, looking at his bottle of Newkie Brown and playing with the label. The worst bit was over.

I then explained that I wanted to sleep with someone, but I wanted the first one to be someone special. Not just anyone. I asked him, "Would you do it?"

I could tell by his face that he wasn't going to. He said really nicely, "I don't think that would be sensible. In the first place, I teach you."

"You don't anymore."

"I might next year."

He said it wouldn't be good from a professional point of view. He also said, "My life is a bit screwed up at the moment. You haven't really chosen a very good person." He had had a relationship which he had messed up and he hadn't got over it yet.

I told him, "The person I love most in the whole world hates me" (Miss Williams).

He said, "In which case, are they worth it?" It was very obvious that he'd said "they" and not "he" as you would expect. I'm sure they all know about it.

"You'll find the right one. And that's not me."

He asked if it was pressure because everyone else was doing it and talking about it?

"No, I just want to."

He said, "The first few times aren't very good. Inexperienced boys do it very quickly and energetically, and women need it to be slow."

He was being very frank.

"So, the answer's definitely 'no,' then?"

"Yes. ... Don't ask that too often."

That was really, really flattering.

He said, "You're young, intelligent, pretty (!). What the fucking hell have you got to worry about?"

"The first time."

I told him it was The Halls Ball on Wednesday and I found myself in the situation, but I couldn't go through with it because it was just anyone.

He said his first few times were crap. He was just so nice about the whole thing.

"If it was so bad the first times, why did you carry on?"

"Well, you see in books, films, and things how good it can be. And also, certain urges." I like that.

I said, "Why do I keep making such an idiot of myself?"

"All the excellent things one does in one's life, one has to pay for by being an idiot sometimes." Then he quickly added, as if he felt he had to, "You haven't made an idiot of yourself, anyway."

I said I thought I'd better be going. We got up.

I said, "Thanks."

He said, "Bye." He winked at me and walked off.

I went to the bus stop. I knew the bus had ended for the night and wasn't going to The Halls, but I looked surprised, as usual, and he drove me to The Halls anyway.

Wednesday 28th June 1989, University

The stud earring in my vagina had started to hurt me yesterday. It hurt a bit to sit down, particularly to cross my legs. Today it still hurt. In the morning, I tried to get it out. It was so tight, it wouldn't budge. It bled a little.

9:15am I knocked on Charlie's door. I had decided he was the only person I could possibly ask to get it out for me. I had woken him up. He sleepily invited me in to sit down. We talked for a minute about The Halls meal last night, then I said the reason why I'd come: "I want you to take an earring out for me ... but it's not in my ear."

"That depends where it is."

I pointed between my legs.

He looked amused and confused and said, "The people I know ..."

I went over to where he was still lying on his bed. He pulled me down. We were kissing. His kiss is not good, but he carried on, so I endured.

I took my leggings and knickers off. He just watched, smiling.

"You don't mind, do you?"

"No."

I lay on the bed and opened my legs out. I really like doing that.

He climbed on the bed and looked to find the earring. He had jeans on only, over red, blue, and green horizontally striped underpants which he'd been sleeping in—same ones he'd been wearing at The Halls Ball.

He tried for ages to get it out. He got hold of the stud and the butterfly and pulled. It hurt so much, I couldn't take it. He said I should go to casualty.

He kept kissing me. I put my clothes back on. He pulled me down on the bed again and started kissing me. This time I tried to think he was Miss Williams to make it more interesting, but it was such a horrible kiss, with his great protruding tongue and all that saliva and stubble.

Then he said, "Will you do me a favour?"

This is the exact sentence he used last week before asking me to give him a blow job.

I said, "No. Goodbye," and left.

Walked to the hospital. Told the lady at the desk what was wrong with me. I was a bit embarrassed. I said, "Between my legs." She didn't laugh. I sat down and waited. After about ten minutes I was called. Service or what? Brilliant.

A nice young nurse took me to a little room. I had to take off my clothes, put on a sort of paper coat, and lie down. She took my temperature. I was alright. A female doctor came. She was quite attractive. She had a look and a poke. I kept imagining how I'd feel if she were my lesbian lover. It wasn't at all exciting, except when she was bending over me and her breast was touching my leg. It felt so warm. It was beautiful.

She couldn't remove the earring, so they fetched a gynaecologist. She was an Asian lady with a black headscarf on. She couldn't believe what I'd done. She asked, "Is this a new fashion in this country?" She tried to remove it with tweezers, but it was so painful.

In the end, they had to give me injections to numb the area. The gynaecologist stuck the needle in four or five times. I was squeezing the nurse's hand tightly and screaming. It was *so* painful. It went numb almost immediately. She tried again. It came out. She had blood on her fingers.

Phew. It was out.

The nurse gave me a prescription. I went to the pharmacy and got some antibiotics. Twice daily until they run out. All that for free. Wow.

Went to Boots. Bought a wooden box as a jewellery box to put Miss Williams's birthday present bracelet in (£5). Bought some paint, to paint it black.

The area where the earring was is still swollen.

Thursday 29th June 1989, University

Bought a piece of red satin to put inside Miss Williams's birthday present jewellery box.

Went to uni. Only slightly nervous about bumping into Mr. Martin. I want him to change his mind.

6:30pm Spud came to see me. He stayed till 7:15pm and only left because I was going out to get a tape back from someone. It's very annoying him staying that long. He invited me over to his room later for a drink with a couple of friends of his.

Spud came to fetch me 10:45pm. We went to his friend's room, drank some Taboo and peach wine, talked about art. I left 11:25pm. Spud walked me back. He kissed me a bit.

Friday 30th June 1989, University > Home

Last day in my room.

Bought *Breakthru* by Queen.

Note from Emily's dad that the bracelet is ready and has arrived. Great.

Dad came to fetch me 8:54pm. I didn't feel very sad leaving.

Got to Emily's house 10:21pm. Her dad showed me the gold bracelet for Miss Williams's birthday present. My feelings were a strange mixture of delight and disappointment. Hard to explain.

Got home 10:50am. I stuck a poster of Miss Williams on the ceiling above my bed. Love it.

Saturday 1st July 1989, Home

Asked Dad to take me into town. When we drove past the engraving place he guessed that was the shop I wanted. He had already guessed that I'd spent all my money on jewellery because I'd had to reveal that Emily's parents didn't pay me at Easter, that I'd bought something instead.

They only do machine engraving. They had seven styles to choose from. They weren't that good, but I can't find anyone else to do it before I have to leave for Italy. It's really upsetting. I hope it turns out alright.

I chose a style called Roman Block, which wasn't too bad, but not as pretty as I wanted. I thought it was going to cost me about £20. It cost £3.40. Emily's dad had told me that machine engravers sometimes get it wrong. I wished I could stand over and watch. I have to fetch it on Tuesday. I asked for 'MISS WILLIAMS' to be engraved on the front.

Got to McDonald's 9:20am. Polly's left! I'm so happy. She used to give me hell about my tattoo. The wages have gone up from £2.20 to £2.38 an hour.

Sunday 2nd July 1989, Home
Spray-painted black a cardboard box for Miss Williams's present. Painted some of the wooden jewellery box black. And made a brilliant cushion for inside out of the red silk.

Tuesday 4th July 1989, Home
Went to the engraving place. I was a bit apprehensive in case they had got it wrong. ... It was great. I was so happy. It's all going right.

Darren Grace drove me home from the McDonald's close. We were talking about driving tests. He said I could have a go in his car if I wanted. We drove to the country lane near the ice rink and swapped seats. I didn't do very well. He thought it was funny. He apologised to me for the jokes he's made about my tattoo, said he hadn't meant to hurt me. Got in about 3am.

Wednesday 5th July 1989, Home

Letter from the bank to say that my £200 overdraft limit has expired AND that I'm £201 overdrawn.

Thursday 6th July 1989, Home

In the evening, I wrapped Miss Williams's birthday present. It took hours. The gold bracelet is sitting on a red silk cushion, in a wooden box, spray-painted black. That is wrapped in yellow tissue paper, then white tissue paper, then the wrapping paper which I designed and Xeroxed, bubble wrap, white cardboard, more tissue paper, white parcel paper, black parcel paper, red parcel paper, brown parcel paper, white tissue paper, and finally red tissue paper.

Friday 7th July 1989, Home > Italy

Got up at 7am. Finished wrapping Miss Williams's birthday present. In the bottom of the outer black box, I put screwed-up newspaper, put the parcel in, then more screwed-up newspaper on top. Taped the box all the way round with black tape.

I stuck six fifty pence stamps on it, put it in a large bag, and left Dad with instructions on when to post it and NOT to look at the address.

Mum took the coach with me to Heathrow.

At customs I was frisked by a lady of about fifty. She touched me all over. Her hands were right on my breasts. I like that so much.

Friday 28th July 1989, Italy

Dad rang. He made sure I knew the travel arrangements for getting to Germany tomorrow.

I checked with him that he had posted my parcel.

"No. I haven't."

I screamed, "DAD!?"

"I suppose Miss Williams is organising your mother's birthday present?"

...

Shit.

He said that Mum was really upset and angry. Louise had forgotten her birthday too.

The End

Two days later ...

... Natasha meets a young woman who will change her life forever.
Read the next instalment ...

Lesbian Crushes and Bulimia:
A Diary on How I Acquired my Eating Disorder
(1989-1990)

Printed in Great Britain
by Amazon

81255658R00139